Out of the Box

Helps for Children's Sunday School Teachers

Abingdon

Nashville

Abingdon's
OUT OF THE BOX
HELPS FOR CHILDREN'S
SUNDAY SCHOOL TEACHERS

ISBN: 0-687-092485-8

Editor: LeeDell Stickler
Production Editor: Lucinda Anderson
Production and Design Manager:
  R. E. Osborne
Design: Adolph C. Lavin
Cover Design: R. E. Osborne
Illustrator: Megan Jeffery

01 02 03 04 05 06 07 08 09 – 10 9 8 7 6 5 4 3

MANUFACTURED IN THE UNITED STATES OF AMERICA

Abingdon Press

Contents

OUT OF THE BOX

Contents *Continues*

Ten Commandments
for Sunday School Teachers

I. Remember that sharing your faith is the reason you are teaching.

II. Pray before and after each class time. Pray at the beginning for guidance and strength; pray at the end to thank God for your courage.

III. Do not wait until Saturday night to plan your lesson.

IV Always arrive before the children; then they will know they are expected.

V. Make children feel welcome and accepted for who they are.

VI. Never belittle any child or cause a child to be embarrassed.

VII. Remember your childhood and how you were treated; don't repeat mistakes that were made with you.

VIII. Be flexible; things rarely turn out as you expect them to. Have Plans B, C, D, and E ready to implement on a moment's notice.

IX. Never lose your temper; discipline with love, not anger.

X. Laugh frequently, but never at the children.

Exercise One:
Sing and Move

Music speaks to the soul of the youngest and the oldest. Why is it that the one part of the teaching lesson that most teachers leave out is the singing activities? Children love to sing and move to music. Take advantage of this natural teaching tool. Children don't care how good your voice is. All they care about is the enthusiasm you exhibit. So get with it. Sing and move!

Wiggle Praise

I *wig - gle, wig - gle, wig - gle, and I praise the Lord! _ I

wig - gle, wig - gle, wig - gle, and I praise the Lord! _ I

wig - gle, wig - gle, wig - gle, and I praise the Lord! _ Al - le - lu - ia!

Additional stanzas: jump, stomp, clap.

WORDS and MUSIC: Linda Ray Miller and Daphna Flegal
© 2000 Cokesbury

Other possible actions you might include are bump, flap, shake, hop, or swivel. Let the children suggest some of their own.

Teaching Sunday School in the New Millennium

by Elinor Ross

Looking into a classroom window today, you might be surprised at what you see. No longer is the teacher front and center facing quiet children seated in straight rows or seated around a little table. In fact, it may be hard to find the teacher at all! Today's teacher is a facilitator, not a director. The teacher is someone who works among the children, assisting them in their endeavors. In today's classroom children are likely to be working or talking together in small groups or with partners as they discover truths for themselves, with the guidance of the teacher. Instead of being teacher-directed, classrooms are child-centered. Children have choices, make decisions, learn to solve their own problems, and work cooperatively. What we know about teaching and learning has changed a great deal over the years, and this article suggests some ideas for keeping up with the times.

Engage the Whole Child

Educators realize how important the connection is between home and school. They try to keep communication open between parents and caregivers. Maintaining positive relations with the children's caregivers at home is important, since children attend Sunday school for only a small portion of the week. Sunday school lessons should spill over into the home, where children put Christian principles into practice during the week. Getting to know the children's parents or significant adult(s) in their lives and sharing your goals with them can extend and reinforce your teachings.

Many Questions, More Answers

Perhaps you remember teachers when you were going to school who insisted that there was only one right answer to a question. For some questions this is true. However, today's teachers realize that there can be different interpretations of the same material depending on each child's experience and perceptions.

Some children may accept the feeding of the people in the story of the loaves and the fish as a miracle that Jesus himself performed. Others may think that the true miracle lay in the eventual voluntary sharing of food among those present. Accept different points of view as long as they are reasonable. Often children present fresh and unexpected insights into the meanings of stories and

Scripture. Listen to what the children say and respond thoughtfully. This is teaching and learning in the new millennium.

Basic Teaching Strategies

Here are some basic strategies that educators have found to be effective for teaching:

• *Show the children.* Modeling is the most effective of all teaching techniques, so model Christian values through your behavior and interactions with others.

• *Review and reinforce.* Start your lessons with a review from the previous week in order to provide continuity, to remind children what the lesson was about, and to inform those not attending last week of the lesson's theme.

• *Reflect and connect.* Conclude each lesson with time for reflection and for asking the children to tell you what they learned—both the information you have taught and how it might connect to their lives.

• *Start with their interests.* Build on the children's curiosity; that is, develop ideas that interest them, and they will be more willing to participate.

• *Be flexible.* Avoid sticking strictly to a predetermined schedule so that you can be responsive to the children as new perceptions and needs arise. Know when to pursue an idea or when to drop it. If your lesson ends early have some sponge activities to soak up the extra time. Sponge activities for younger children could be fingerplays or songs. Older students might read an extra story, take a quiz or play a game.

Discoveries Not Lectures

Use an interactive approach as you present the content of the lesson to the children, whether you are studying Bible stories or values. Ask questions while reading or telling so that the

children can think and respond. Get the children actively involved in the lesson instead of expecting them to listen passively as you present the material. Ask such questions as, What was God saying to Noah when he sent the rainbow?or Why do you think the bush was burning?

Although time may be limited, be sure to explore meanings. Too often we rush through the lesson without giving the children time to think about what the material means to them. Guide their thinking by asking, "What does this story mean to you? How might it change the way you treat other people? What might you do differently this week because of this lesson? What one thing did you learn today that is really important to remember?" Taking time to reflect on the lesson makes it more meaningful and long-lasting.

Reflection

How can children reflect? Small children reflect through discussion or simple drawings. Go over the story; then ask the children the simple question, What does this mean? and wait for their answers. Listen to their responses for clues about what they have gained; there are no right or wrong answers. The children's reflections show what the story or lesson means to each of them.

Older children may want to keep journals—collections of brief notations where they can express their reaction to the lesson. They can make journals themselves, choosing covers

8

from colored construction paper, folding them in half, and decorating them. A few sheets of folded paper can be stapled inside for the children to write on at the conclusion of each lesson. Journals should be kept in the Sunday school classroom so that the children can add to them each time they attend. Or ask, "What does this story or lesson make you feel like doing?" Possible responses are drawing, singing, or even dancing.

Teaching Materials
As a Sunday school teacher you are probably provided with lesson materials that may include a teacher book, student materials, stickers, posters, and music. These materials support the theme of the lesson and provide relevant activities. But remember that these materials are created by people who don't know your children. They may know *some* children, but not yours. Feel free to supplement the materials with those of your own, or provide alternative activities if you feel something else is more appropriate. But be sure that your alternatives are appropriate for your students' age range and understanding level, and that the alternatives are consistent with the lesson and the theological approach of the materials and your church. Teachers in public schools frequently modify lesson plans and adapt their lessons to suit the needs and interests of their children. They are not bound by the lessons in their manuals, and neither are you.

Learning By Seeing
Many children learn through touching and moving so object lessons are still appealing to them. Bringing in a bird's feather or a seashell or a piece of driftwood and examining the intricacies of the object encourage children to marvel at God's handiwork. Whenever possible, find tangible objects to enrich your lesson. Even though older children try to maintain a sophisticated attitude, they still enjoy learning through their senses.

Developmentally Appropriate Practices
Remember, children are capable of different things at different ages. Educators call these "developmentally appropriate practices." These terms simply mean that the children are "acting their age." Know children's development well enough (refer to the chart on pages 38–39 of this workbook) to have reasonable expectations for teaching activities and learning goals for the children at each age. Don't expect nursery school children to

cooperate well with other children, they are much too self-centered. Younger elementary children can reflect on a lesson, but they will not often agree on what the lesson means. Older children may read, write about, and discuss the stories; they often like to write in journals.

Learning Styles

As you keep in mind the developmental stages of your children, also remember that children learn through looking, listening, talking, moving, touching, doing, drawing, and writing. Although educators agree that children learn in many different ways, teachers often rely heavily on the telling-listening teaching style. This style is easy to fall back on. It requires very few supplies, and cleanup is non–existent. Teachers may feel as if the goal of the lesson has been accomplished once the information has been imparted. There are at least seven learning styles, however (see "Seven Ways of Knowing," pages 44-45). You may enjoy trying some or all of them.

Many children fail to get the message if it is delivered in only one way. They need to be actively involved to absorb the meaning of the lesson. Educators often call this process hands-on or active learning. Hands on means involving the whole child, using art, music, contemplation, cooperative learning, listening, drawing, painting, molding, constructing, role playing, dramatic reading, and writing.

Don't take too much time with any one learning style. Try not to spend the entire class time making a mural of God's creatures, for example. Also you shouldn't try to get all learning styles into every lesson. Just make sure that you don't rely heavily on only one style while ignoring the rest. Vary your teaching strategies.

Classroom Management

As you know, you can't send misbehaving Sunday school children to the principal. We offer praise for any kind of good behavior. We try to ignore bad behavior as much as possible. Many children simply want recognition. Children usually misbehave for one of four reasons: they are bored, they are frustrated, they don't know what's expected of them, or they want your attention. There are many ways to address all these in non-threatening ways.

1. *Mutual responsibility.* When children know what is expected, they can take much of the responsibility for appropriate and non-appropriate behavior. Set the goals together. Ask the children what they want to learn, and make plans together. (How do we want to learn?) Ask the children what rules they think are important. Children who have a say in what and how they learn are more likely to participate, enjoy the class, and benefit from the lesson.

2. *Comfortable routines.* Children are more comfortable when they know what to expect. Establish procedures that work well with your group, but also allow for some flexibility. Special occasions or religious holidays may call for activities that do not fit into the routine. You may sometimes want to do such things as take a field trip in order to look at the stained glass windows in the sanctuary. But on the whole, devise a basic pattern to your class time and stick with it.

3. *Appropriate environment.* Even though you may have little time for decorating your room, and perhaps little space as well, you should display relevant materials as attractively as you can. Classrooms reflect the teaching and learning that occurs, and your Sunday school classroom needs to reflect what the children are learning and doing. New and different ways to handle or look at information heighten anticipation as the children arrive. The room environment can say "Sunday school is important" and "I love you enough to prepare our space."

4. *Age-level appropriate furniture.* Is it the correct size for your students? Is it clean and in good condition? While you as a teacher may not choose to paint or clean,

you can be an advocate for your students with the church administration.

5. *Child-produced decor.* Decorate with student art or crafts. Children may occasionally create something to accompany the lesson. Having their own work on display raises the children's self-esteem and gives them a sense of ownership of their space.

6. *My own special place.* Children like to feel special and you can help them do so by taking a photograph of each child, mounting it, and placing it on a bulletin board.

In Conclusion
Educators have learned a great deal about teaching and learning from observing children and teachers in action. What was "good enough" ten years ago isn't good enough anymore. There are too many options vying for the time of our children. Sunday school should be a high-touch place where children can find love and acceptance by being God's children.

Dr. Elinor P. Ross is professor of curriculum and instruction at Tennessee Technological University. She is a member of First United Methodist Church in Cookeville, Tennessee, where she teaches Sunday school.

Exercise Two:
Can You Remember?

_____ : Who was Time Magazine's Man of the Year in 1995?

_____ : What motion picture won the Best Picture Academy award in 1985?

_____ : What football team won the Super Bowl in 1991?

_____ : Name one book that appeared on the New York Times' bestseller list for fiction in January of 1999?

_____ : Who won the Nobel Peace Prize in 1997?

_____ : Who represented your state in the Miss America contest this past year?

_____ : Who was your best friend when you were in the first grade?

_____ : What was your favorite book to be read aloud when you were in elementary school?

_____ : Who was your first Sunday school teacher?

_____ : Who taught you to ride a bicycle?

_____ : Can you name an Old Testament Bible story?

_____ : Can you name a New Testament Bible story?

_____ : Can you name one of Jesus' disciples?

_____ : What Bible verse can you say by heart?

12

Exercise Three:
But First . . .

Remind yourself about the supreme importance of what you are about to do. Take some time to consider what the Bible has to say about teaching. For each of these passages:

1. Read the Scripture.
2. Meditate on the Scripture and listen for God's word.
3. Discuss the Scripture with someone else, if you wish.
4. Write a word or phrase (not sentences or paragraphs) that summarizes what this Scripture says to you about being a teacher.

Ephesians 4:11–16 _____

2 Timothy 2:1–2 _____

1 Corinthians 4:1–2 _____

1 Corinthians 16:13–14 _____

1 Corinthians 1:26–31 _____

2 Timothy 2:15 _____

Colossians 1:9–12 _____

James 3:1 _____

Matthew 18:5–7 _____

Luke 6:39–40 _____

Proverbs 4:5–9 _____

Titus 2:1 _____

Philippians 4:13 _____

End your time of spiritual preparation with a prayer. Ask God to be with you as you plan and as you teach. Ask God to help you remember that God will bless your efforts and what God has called you to do.

Planning for Teaching

Main Idea of the Lesson:
(Write the Main Idea—found near the beginning of the lesson plan in the Teacher book—in your own words.)

Bible Verse(s):

1. Get Started
(Relates to the theme of the lesson. The first child to arrive can begin alone.)

2. Review
(Helps the children remember what they did last week or "catch up" if they were absent. May be a part of the arrival activity.)

3. Present New Material
(Gives basic information for today's learning—Bible story, customs from Bible times, relevant contemporary situations, and so forth.)

4. "Set" the Learning
(Provides opportunities for each child to learn in his or her own creative way. Remember the various learning styles.)

5. Reflect and Worship
(Provides a time for children to think about what they have learned and about what they will do in their own lives and to praise God.)

What to Do When There's Only a Few

The success of Sunday school teachings does not depend on numbers or ages. Many churches are asking, "What can we do with so few? What kinds of Christian education events will nourish our members in faith formation? How can Sunday school be meaningful when there are only two or three children in our whole area?"

One example of effective Christian education occurred in a church where a sixth grade boy helped teach several younger children. This boy settled a two-year-old on his lap as he told the Bible story to another preschooler. Later an adult led the younger ones in songs and roleplays while the sixth grader devised an intricate matching game to share with his parents.

This church didn't doubt their realness or their ability to provide Christian education to members of differing age groups. They would never be likely to have large classes in this isolated region, but there is no doubt that the Sunday school there is vital and effective. You can start a Sunday school or revitalize a lagging one with careful planning and congregational cooperation. Let's look at the one room concept.

One Room Sunday School

Many smaller churches today are using the one room Sunday school concept. This concept reflects the rural public schools structure in which all classes from kindergarten through eighth grade are taught in one room. The essential needs for a one room Sunday school are

- Space: open, in either a fellowship hall or large classroom;
- Teachers: at least one adult, although two would be great;
- Students: potentially all children and youth of the church or community;
- Support: a congregation that knows what is going on and provides the simple supplies needed. The teacher gets a break once in awhile.

This type of teaching encourages attendance. It does not complain when learning centers are left up in the fellowship hall or crayons are put in the wrong cupboard.

Curriculum materials have been developed for the one room Sunday school. One resource, available from Cokesbury, is called ONE ROOM SUNDAY SCHOOL. These materials are purchased in a kit and include a Teacher Book, a reproducible activities book, a class resource, and a cassette. The reproducible activities provide learning activities appropriate for children ages three through middle school. Teachers select and reproduce the needed pages according to the age levels of the students. Guidelines in the Teacher Book help the teacher to facilitate learning for students across an age span of several years. The Class Pak includes maps, teaching pictures, games, charts, and activities for all ages.

Since such a class involves a wide age range of students, children do not do the same things at the same times. Gathering in a conversation and worship circle gives everyone an opportunity to hear the Bible story or lesson. Learning centers then accommodate students of all ages, reinforcing the story or lesson through learning activities. These centers may include tables. Students can stand around tables while working. The centers may also include a circle of carpet squares in a secluded corner for learning a new song; a study corner; a puzzle nook. The teacher here would serve as a facilitator rather than a dispenser of facts. Older students would assist younger ones. Students would choose activities that are right for themselves, so that each child could work at his or her own ability and interest level.

This is not an "open classroom." The teacher will give assignments to small groups of children who are either unwilling or unmotivated to choose activities. The teacher will also plan for closing minutes when the class shares its learnings, checks understandings, and affirms relationships. Youth may become assistant teachers in this kind of learning setting. But they also need opportunities for discussion and reflection at their own level. Small churches are accustomed to working together and to planning events that include everyone. One room Sunday school is an extension of that familiar pattern.

After-School Programs

Thousands of after-school programs are springing up around the country. Most appeal to youngsters with working parents or to families who have no attachment to Sunday church programs. The most successful after-school programs begin with carefully crafted goals and guidelines, training for teachers and facilitators, and a wise choice of curriculum and methods.

Decide first what you really want to do. Reach out to unchurched children? provide care for latchkey children for a few hours? develop a children's choir? provide an extra or alternative session of Sunday school? build community among diverse populations? When you know your primary goal, build guidelines for getting it done. Consider times, dates, place, transportation, leadership, and specific expectations for teachers and students.

Plan nourishing snacks for hungry students. Offer active learning activities for restless, growing bodies. Provide exciting stories and Bible work that children can easily apply to day-to-day living in school and at home. Listen to children; this may be the only one-on-one relating a youngster will have all day. Show your own discipleship and share your faith. Sometimes these children have no experience in church; you will be teaching values, etiquette, and personal relationships as one part of the curriculum. Love and teach all the children who come. God will take it from there.

Adapted from
"What to Do When There's Only a Few"
© 2000 Cokesbury

OUT OF THE BOX

One Size Doesn't Fit All

Anyone who has ever bought an article of clothing labeled "One Size Fits All" knows that it doesn't. The same is true about Sunday school curriculum. So what do you do when the curriculum isn't a perfect fit?

Your class time is shorter than the allotted time for the printed lesson.
- Shorten the lesson. Don't try to do everything that is written there. Be selective. A rule of thumb is: Have an arrival activity, the Bible story activity, a craft activity, a closing worship activity.

Your class time is longer than the allotted time for the printed lesson.
- Choose activities from the alternatives. (Most curriculum offers alternative activities.)
- Let the children be involved in planning their own worship time.
- Use learning centers with supplementary activities for the children to choose from.

Your class doesn't have room for active games, or you don't want the children revved up prior to worship.
- Leave out the game and substitute an art or reflection activity.
- See if there is a less active way to play the game.

You don't have time to gather all the needed supplies, or your church doesn't have a budget that will cover unusual supplies.
- Choose a different craft activity.
- Adapt the craft activity to fit the supplies you do have.
- Substitute a different craft activity that doesn't need as many supplies.

You have a small number of children, making some activities difficult.
- Don't try to do group games with only two or three children. Create board games or let them create their own kind of Trivial Pursuit.

You have an ADHD child in your class.
- Avoid super active games that will set off this child.
- Keep your class structure basically the same each Sunday.
- Seek a parent or a youth to be an aid whose primary goal is to supervise this child.

You have a child who knows more than all the others (usually a pastor's child).
- Don't let this child answer all the questions.
- Involve this child in helping to prepare the room or the lesson.
- Give this child special responsibilities.

You have a special needs child in your room.
- Do not plan activities that will make this child feel uncomfortable.
- Adapt activities so that this child can participate where possible.

You have all boys or all girls in your class.
- Choose a variety of activities. Don't choose all active games for a class of girls or all writing and creating activities for a class of boys.

You have a wide scope of ability levels in your class. You want the children to learn Bible verses, and the curriculum provides a memory verse each week. But some children have difficulty memorizing.
- Use games to teach Bible verses.
- Do not make the learning of Bible verses competitive so that children who don't memorize well will feel less than a part of the class.

You have children who are sensitive about their size/weight/glasses or any other distinguishing feature.
- Most Sunday school material avoids putting children in embarrassing situations, but if you feel any activity or project will affect one of your children in an adverse way, choose another activity.

The children in your church dress up in fairly expensive clothing for Sunday school. The curriculum you are using often suggests messy craft activities. You are afraid to try them with the children.
- Substitute a less messy craft for the one suggested by the curriculum.
- Declare a "Messy Sunday" and send letters home to parents telling them to dress the children in more washable clothing for the time you will be using that activity.
- Provide garbage bags with head and arm holes cut so that the children can slip the bags on over their clothing.

Growing in Christian Faith

Your Christian faith becomes a reality when the stories of the Bible and your personal experiences of God's love and grace inspire you to love God and to trust God's guidance as you make decisions about living each day.

Learning the Bible

When asked "What is the most important thing in creating a Christian foundation?" people respond, "the Bible." The Bible is the place where most persons begin the development of their Christian faith. It is very true that as a person learns the stories of the faith and becomes familiar with God's teachings, he or she also develops a deeper understanding of the purposes of Scripture. Through these experiences persons learn to recognize God's call. But knowing the Bible is not enough.

Accepting God's Grace

In fact, many people who are not Christians know more about the Bible than many of us who are Christians. Knowledge of the Bible doesn't create Christians. The belief that the words of the Bible are God's message to us is what impels a person to become a Christian. The recognition that God's love shown through Jesus Christ is real and the acceptance of God's saving grace offered through Jesus Christ as a special gift is what enables one to become the person God created him or her to be.

Growing in the Faith

Christians want to learn more about Jesus' teachings. They want to discover the gifts of God that come through the Holy Spirit. Christians want to learn more about what it means to live as a person of faith. Christians are not satisfied simply to know the Bible and to believe in God. Christians want to grow in their understanding of God's purposes and want their relationship with God to grow deeper day by day and year by year.

Becoming a Part of a Community

Christians recognize that the ability to grow in relationship to God is possible only in fellowship with other Christians. Although

Christians value time alone in prayer and communion with God, Christians also welcome times to praise God and give thanks for God's gracious love and care in worship and prayer with one another. Through the Christian relationship that develops, Christians strengthen one another so that they are able to carry their experience of God's presence and love into the activities of their everyday lives.

Answering God's Call

Living a Christian life does not come automatically and is not a one-time thing. Christian living comes through study, worship, and learning together. It continues throughout one's life. Sunday school is a beginning place for children to learn what it means to answer God's call. When children learn to follow the example of Jesus Christ, they become Christian examples, revealing the love of God through their own actions at home, at work, at play, at church, or anywhere they may be.

Pray With and for the Children

Pray with the children. Use simple prayers, perhaps those suggested in your curriculum resources. Or simply pray from your heart in words that the children will understand. Most important of all, do not forget to help the children learn to pray. Provide times for silent prayer. Encourage the children to pray aloud, but do not force them to do so.

Silent Prayers

Taking time to think silently about God and to talk to God in their hearts is a valuable experience for children.

Musical Prayers

Look for prayer songs in your curriculum materials. Talk about the words of the songs before you sing them. Encourage the children to gather reverently to sing when they hear the music begin to play.

Litanies

Help the children write their own prayer litanies—responsive prayers. Have the children list things they are thankful for, people they want to pray for, times when they need to feel that God is near, and so forth. Then make their lists into litanies by having the children repeat a single learned line such as "God, hear our prayer" after each item on the list is read aloud.

Art Prayers

Let the children write the words of their prayers into pictures. Perhaps the words will form the outline of a shape like a church or a butterfly. Perhaps the words can be written inside a cutout of the child's own handprint. Perhaps the words of the prayer can be the leaves on a tree in a storm. Some pictures can become prayer cards for the family to use on the table at home.

Sentence Prayers

Help children learn to pray aloud in groups. Begin with the experience of sentence prayers. Let each student say one sentence that names something he or she wants to pray about. But remember, do not force children to pray.

Prayer Calendars, Pockets, and Chains

Have the children write the things they want to pray for on a calendar for the week. Or they could write their prayers on strips of paper and loop them together to make a chain. Prayer strips can also be put into a paper pocket made from construction paper. Each day during the week, the child can check the calendar, pull one strip from the prayer pocket, or cut one link off the chain for a suggestion for how to pray that day.

Prayer: A Natural Part of Ordinary Expression

- When the children are excited and having fun, say: "Let's stop a moment and say thank you to God for providing such a wonderful place for us to come and have fun together." Let the children shout,"Thank you, God!" in unison.

- When a child is sad or having a bad day, show your concern by saying a short prayer with the child. "God, you know Joey doesn't feel good today. Help him remember that you love him even when things are not going so well."

- When a bird lands on the window sill, encourage all the children to thank God for creating the beautiful birds.

- When a classmate is ill, lead the children in praying for God's comfort and healing for the one who is sick.

- Have the children write something they are thankful for or need help with and put the slips of paper in a basket. Pass the basket around and have each child pick out a slip and pray out loud for one another. (Praying as a group helps children who are shy.)

- Bring in the local newspaper. Have the children cut out articles or headlines about events to pray about. Make a collage. Develop a litany from the collage with the response: Lord, hear our prayer.

- Have the children go around your church with a tape recorder or pad and pencil and get prayer requests. Share and pray as a group.

- During the closing time of your class, have children share sentence prayers. Start the prayer and allow the children to finish.

- During the prayer time, have younger children recall a recent experience of joy or sadness and share it. Verbalize these experiences as prayers. Soon children will be able to pray on their own.

- Let the children write a litany on a particular theme related to what the class is studying and use it in worship in the class.

Exercise Four:

Praying For You, Class

My Class Prayer List	My Class Prayer List

OUT OF THE BOX

Teaching for Commitment

As a children's Sunday school teacher, you have the opportunity to help children know about Jesus Christ. You are also called to nurture and encourage them to say "yes" to Christ's invitation to follow him. And you are called to help them as they continue to make commitments throughout their lives to become more faithful in their daily living.

We enter the world as infants, part of God's plan for creation. It is God's intention that we grow and mature throughout our lifetimes.

Our faith development might be compared to the development of a tree. A tree is a whole tree whether it is five feet tall or fifty feet tall. The same elements are present in roots, trunk, bark, branches, and leaves of trees. But the fifty-foot tree has these elements in greater quantities. And the size and shape of the tree changes as it grows. Likewise, a child who is five years old has faith, but an adult of fifty years has an expanded and stronger faith. We are whole persons. Our growth in faith is related to our growth in all areas of our lives—body, mind, spirit, and emotions.

We must be careful, however, not to conclude that faith commitment will automatically develop or that it is a neatly arranged package we can manipulate. We are created in the image of God, but that image may become distorted. We need to let ourselves be forgiven and reshaped so that we reflect the image of

God more clearly. And when we wander astray, we need to be turned around.

Nurture and conversion are both essential in our Christian faith development. Nurture means to feed, nourish, or support during various stages of growth. Conversion means turning around or changing in character, form, or function. In the Christian church we think of conversion in more specific terms: as spiritual change from self-centeredness to Christ-centeredness.

Some of us experience conversion as God's grace coming to us like gentle spring rains. At various periods in our faith development we become more aware of God's grace in our lives. At such times we make quiet, firm decisions to make a deeper commitment to Jesus Christ. For others conversion may seem more like lightning or thunder. God breaks our old life patterns, and we welcome God's grace. Paul, on the road to Damascus, had such an experience.

A common misunderstanding of conversion is that we are transformed from a state of turmoil to a peaceful, tranquil state. This transformation does not necessarily happen. When we accept Jesus Christ as our Savior, he shatters our self-centered and clouded ways of viewing reality. Christ demands a total response of heart, mind, will, and lifestyle. We are called to be open to the transforming power of God throughout our lives. As we do this, we begin to see things in our lives and in the world that are not in harmony with what Christ is calling us to be and to do. In reality conversion often brings *discomfort* instead of *comfort.*

While God does not promise us a life of comfort as a result of conversion, God does come to us as Comforter through the Holy Spirit. While God prods us, God also sustains us and guides us as we seek to be faithful to his will for our lives.

Whatever the nature of our conversion—gradual or sudden, gentle or earthshaking—it does bring us to a new focus and a new power for life. We become new creatures in Christ.

This new life requires not only conversion but nurture. We need to be nourished in the Christian faith in order to become aware of Jesus Christ and to make commitments to follow him. And we need nurture throughout our lives so that we continue to grow in our faith.

Nurturing for Commitment
Worship
Worship is a setting for both nurture and commitment. Worship is one of the primary ways we remember and express our Christian faith. We gather as a community of faith around the baptismal font, the Communion table, the Holy Bible, the cross, and the altar to confess and praise. Together, as a community of faith, we remember the biblical story. We make commitments to God as the biblical stories are imprinted on our lives. Then we depart to live and share the faith story entrusted to us.

Study
While weekly corporate worship is a continuing reenactment of the biblical story, Christian education helps us know this story and make it our own.

Studying the Bible involves three related but different approaches. In one approach we study for information. We seek knowledge of what is in the Bible and an understanding of its message. In a sense the biblical story is imprinted in our lives. In a second approach we study primarily for formation. In this approach we study thoughtfully, seeking to let the Word shape or form our lives. We respond to God to be shaped and formed into the image of Christ. In the third approach we are open to transformation. There are times when the Scriptures may strike a response in us for change. Sometimes our own life experiences call for a radical change—a turning around.

Explore the use of all three approaches to Bible study in any one class session. How you go about Bible study will depend on the unit of study, the age level, and the needs of your specific group. Studying for information is easier to recognize, since it includes being able to repeat and use facts and ideas. Studying for formation and transformation is more related to personal meanings and applications to one's spiritual growth. You can plan for activities such as writing, creating, sharing in small groups, praying, or singing. You can also encourage students to read their Bibles at home and to ask God to help them live by it.

Relationships

While instruction in the Christian faith is essential, relationships are just as important. Christian teachings have meaning when we hear them in a faith community where the love of God is evident in the lives of people. Religion is caught as much as it is taught. Persons are nurtured toward commitment as they hear faith experiences of others and share their experiences.

You can help nourish your students by providing warm, caring relationships in the classroom. You can also encourage class members to participate in areas of congregational life other than Sunday school. Such opportunities might include fellowship suppers, service projects, recreation, worship, workshops and programs, mission studies, and retreats.

Spiritual Guidance

Spiritual guidance provides insight and support for making and living faith commitments. We all need spiritual guidance to help us clarify and interpret where we are in our Christian faith. We also need suggestions for new possibilities for growth. And we need challenge and support to help us make changes in our lives so that we grow more Christlike.

Opportunities for transformation abound! You are called to help provide spiritual guidance for the children in your group. Much guidance can be given as you teach the group. But there will be times when you work with individuals. You may sense that a person is ready to make his or her first public commitment to Christ, for example. Another person may be ready to move to a higher level of commitment and may need someone to listen, support, and guide. You can often be that person. There may be times when you will want to refer a child to your pastor or to a layperson who has experience in giving spiritual direction.

The following section provides some suggestions to help you feel more comfortable when you face opportunities to provide spiritual guidance.

Making a Commitment
Share Your Own Faith

Share portions of your faith story with your class to illustrate certain points. Once you do this, others will be more open to talking about their faith journeys.

Use Appropriate Language

Perhaps one of the reasons for our reluctance is that we do not have a ready vocabulary for sharing our faith. Teachers need a variety of words or phrases to use in different situations. This vocabulary is essential for working with persons of different age levels, and is also helpful in working with individuals within a specific age level, since all persons are not at the same place in their faith development.

Choose some words and phrases that seem comfortable for you and appropriate for the child with whom you are talking. Eventually, you will become comfortable using these words in talking with both your class and with individuals.

Young children model their behaviors after adults who are special and significant to them. You can help them know Jesus as a loving, caring person whom they will want to be like. You might use phrases such as "being like Jesus," "doing what Jesus taught," and "being a friend of Jesus" in your teaching.

Elementary children need to feel accepted and needed. With this age level you might speak of "following Jesus," "becoming a disciple of Jesus," "giving your heart to God," "accepting God's love which saves us," or "joining with other followers of Jesus."

Youth often question and doubt the faith that has been shared with them through others. This skepticism indicates that they are searching for a deeper commitment. Help them see that commitment to Christ makes Christianity distinctively different from other religions.

Some commitment phrases to use with youth are "choosing Christ," "giving your life to Christ," "making a commitment to Christ," "following Christ," or "accepting Christ as your personal Savior."

Be Sensitive

Show the boys and girls in your class that you are interested in their growth in faith. Be a good listener. Make comments or ask questions as appropriate.

If you sense a class member is ready to make a personal commitment to Christ, talk privately with the person. If she or he is not ready to pursue the conversation, do not push. When the time is right, the person may return to you because you have shown concern and sensitivity. In the meantime listen, care about, love, and pray for that person.

One of the greatest moments a teacher can have is when someone asks how to make a commitment or shares his or her need to make a deeper commitment to God. It is important to listen to what the student is saying, allow her or him to use words that are comfortable and, at the appropriate time, encourage him or her to make a commitment to God in prayer. There is no one way to encourage commitment. People do not need us in order to make a commitment to Jesus Christ, but our presence at this time in their lives can be a special gift. Sometimes people want someone with them at this pivotal time. Our role can be to help them mark their decision that "on this particular day with this person I made a commitment" to follow God, ask Christ into my heart, listen to the Spirit's leading, or begin a life of discipleship.

In the church we nurture children for commitment through worship, relationships, study, and guidance. Personal commitment to Christ brings change—sometimes sudden, sometimes gradual. Nurture is essential to prepare children for conversion or change, or to help children grow in their faith.

You are called to be a teacher—a spiritual friend and guide to help the children grow and accept the power and love of Jesus Christ for their lives. Rely on God, and you will find the power and understanding you need.

Adapted from "Teaching for Commitment"
© 2000 Cokesbury

The Spiritual Life of Sunday School Teachers

by Donna Schaper

In a way there is nothing unique about the spiritual life of Sunday school teachers. We are all children of God and have certain coordinates in common. We live, we die, we are baptized, and we enjoy Communion. But everything is different for a person who spends time teaching children about God. The responsibility is enormous. The work is all underground. And the pay-off comes long after we're not around to see it.

The Rewards Come Later.

Let's address the last issue first. If you require immediate gratification, don't teach Sunday school. Sunday school teachers are more like a compost pile than anything else: What is happening now is much less important than what

happens later. Each of us adds a leaf or a grass clipping to the growing Christian, year by year. We turn over our composition to give it some air. Then we leave the pile–and the black magic that grows food doesn't appear until another dozen or so people have had a hand in developing the soil. Some people may even add poison to the pile–or may already have done so. We may not be just builders, but also re-builders; sometimes we may have to take something out to make the pile healthy again.

By the time a child finally remembers to thank us for what we taught him in third grade, he may be living in Minneapolis, while we are living in Miami! When a child we have taught faces her husband's cancer with hope and dignity, we may have already gone to our grave. The rewards are not immediate; instead, they are deep, long, and layered.

The Work Is Underground.

The second issue, that of underground work, is equally invisible and equally powerful. We have to know something in order to teach. That acquisition of knowledge takes work. What could happen in a student's life that you would be pleased to hear about in a few years, or that would make you feel proud of having a part in the child's success? What parts of the great story does the child need to hear first to understand the rest? Clearly, Mark should come before Acts, and Genesis before Judges. Love precedes judgement, just as Pentecost precedes the Trinity.

Teachers are compost makers and bricklayers. We have to get the right brick down first so that the next brick will fit on top.

The Responsibility Is Enormous.

The third issue, that of responsibility for the work we do, is the most difficult. Management experts are convinced that very simple things are involved in what we call work, but the simplicity of these things may prove to be our complexity. Just do these things, they say: Show up on time, do what you say you'll do, finish what you start, and say please and thank you. Delegate everything except those things in the area of your particular genius—keep that all to yourself. If there is a particular biblical story that you understand deeply, don't let anyone else tell it. If there is a difficult child only you can handle, hang onto that kid. If there is a story you don't understand, make sure you get a good tutor or curriculum guide—or have the child join the next grade that day. If there is a child you have difficulty dealing with, give that child to someone else for tending. Otherwise the simple manners of work prevail: Get there and do what you say you are going to do.

These management experts argue that teachers, like everybody else, need to escape from the complexity of too much happening, not enough time to think and learn, too little security, not enough opportunity, and too few resources with too little leverage. We need to create enough personal genius in our classrooms that we can teach and students can learn. We must either ignore the political problems in the church or Sunday school or solve them. We must take charge of our room, our hour, and our students' hour. If we can't have what we

need in order to teach well, then we should quit.

Many have found lifelong comfort in the words of the Heidelberg catechism, for example: "What is your only comfort in life and death? That I belong—body and soul, in life and in death—not to myself but to my faithful Savior Jesus Christ." We are better fed by knowing to whom we belong than by anything we put into our mouths. It is up to teachers to make sure that children know about God. When we starve our children from knowledge of God, we are abusing them spiritually and setting them up for failure in the most important area of their lives.

That's why it is so important for teachers to work at teaching. The stakes are enormous. To be successful a teacher must own her or his own gifts and talents and claim responsibility as a teacher.

Teachers who are ready to assume the responsibility of leading children to God and who are prepared for the deep underground and infrastructure nature of this work have only one more job. That is to be learners of the Spirit themselves. "You, then, that teach others, will you not teach yourself?" (Romans 2:21)

"The human race becomes more and more a race between education and catastrophe," said H. G. Wells in 1920. If only Wells could see children carrying guns into school! If only he could watch the blank faces of children when someone asks them a question about the Bible!

Some children will find their way with or without teachers. Some will learn what they need to survive simply because they have no other choice. On more than one occasion I have marveled at how good drug dealers are at math and at organizing small businesses. They are learning—just learning in an anti-social way.

We Must Own the Land.

In order to teach we must own our territory. We must be in charge. We must know God first ourselves before we teach children about God. Whether we are honoring our bodies; praying in simple, old-fashioned ways; taking quiet time to meditate; saying what we need as human beings, mothers, fathers, teachers, and church members, whether we are keeping the Sabbath or skipping church—no matter what part of the Spirit we are practicing, we become teachers by becoming learners of the Spirit. We

are living the Spirit that we teach about, whether we are giving testimony, managing a difficult group of children, forgiving someone who has disappointed us, or healing someone who is burned out or being used.

The following story illustrates how responsibility, work, and spiritual preparation are linked:

While I was volunteering in the six-year-old group at our family summer camp, I heard an experienced teacher read a story about a candy cane. She skipped the part that tells that the candy cane symbolizes the stripes and wounds on Jesus' back. She only explained that the 'J' stands for 'Jesus' and that viewed upside-down, the cane looks like a shepherd's crook. She had decided that the children were too young to hear about the blood of the stripes on Jesus' back. Noticing that she had skipped a page, one boy demanded that it be read too. The teacher read the page, but left out the gory parts. But the boy kept asking, "Why did they kill Jesus?" And he wanted to know who did it.

This teacher answered the hardest question in Christian theology by saying, "Some people are really mean. God loves even the mean ones.

But when meanness overtakes a person, he or she does horrible things, like killing Jesus." She went on to say "Unfortunately, Tommy, each one of us has a little bit of anger in us."

She then turned the children's attention to times when they had been angry with each other on the playground. The children were able to find anger, forgiveness, and love in the hands of an expert teacher. She had prepared to lay her brick for that day. She had done her work. And when the lesson became more complicated than she had expected, she was able to teach out of her own spirit.

Preparing our spirits is as important as preparing our lessons. Otherwise, we'll skip a page. And the children will know it.

Donna Schaper is a minister in the United Church of Christ and the author of several books, including Sabbath Sense (Cowley Press) and Calmly Plotting the Resurrection (United Church Press).

Prayer Times for Teachers

by Patricia Ann Meyers

How can you strengthen your teaching ministry? Here's how one church provides a solid foundation for its teachers.

It's Sunday morning. You are a teacher surrounded by twenty fifth and sixth graders, all vying for your attention at the same time. On your lips is a gentle smile. A sense of peace and calm pervades you, even though you may have pulled a "Saturday night special" to be here at all. Such an attitude can be the result of doing what we do at 9:20 every Sunday morning. We have ten minutes of quiet prayer time for all our Sunday school teachers before they go to class.

Our Sunday school begins for our children's division with an opening exercise we call "Let's Get Started" (LGS). Children of Sunday school teachers and choir members and others who arrive early go to the LGS room. They are met by our diaconal minister and a few youth who provide games, learning centers, and projects to help the children make the transition from "getting here" to "being here." While parents are free to do their last-minutes preparations for Sunday school or worship, they know that their children are safe, content, and positively engaged.

The final preparation for our Sunday school teachers is ten minutes of quiet prayer in a room away from the children. Low lights, a cup of coffee, a chance to share with other teachers, and then praying for each teacher and student silently and corporately contribute to the atmosphere of peace. Our teachers' prayer time gives teachers that final assurance that God is indeed with them as they share the Word of God with others. It reminds them that they do not teach alone.

Following their prayer time, the teachers join the children in LGS, where the children have been singing, sharing birthdays and other important information, and learning worship skills. Teachers, aides, and students then walk to their classes together, really prepared for Sunday school.

Prayer time for teachers is so simple. It happens because the work area on education made it a priority. The work area chairperson is in the prayer room and helps the teachers prepare their hearts and minds for the tasks ahead. She does so by modeling the behavior we think is good for teachers and students alike in prayer, practicing the presence of God. The Sunday school superintendent, the custodian, the diaconal minister, and the youth helpers all help to make this time possible.

Since we started the prayer time, we can tell the difference in the stress and noise level of both teachers and students. Parents also seem to feel good about this added dimension to the Sunday school. We feel that our Sunday school is more effective now. We use all our time and talents more efficiently, and everyone feels better. We started our teachers' prayer time several years ago and we can definitely say, "It works for us!"

Adapted from *Leader in the Church School Today*, Winter 1989-90, © 1989 Graded Press.

What's Your Spiritual Type?

Have you ever attended a worship service where you felt that you didn't "fit?" The worship service itself was interesting and had all the necessary parts, but when you left you simply didn't feel spiritually nurtured? Then perhaps the worship service did not address your particular spiritual needs.

In the study of the different styles and forms of worship, an interesting discovery has been made. Most of us were aware of it long before it became official, simply by the churches we chose and the kind of worship that is predominant in that congregation. There are four predominant spiritual types: Head, Heart, Mystic, and Kingdom. When you hear the descriptions, you will probably recognize yourself easily. Read each of the statements below. Put a check in the box that most closely fits the way you feel. There may be shades of difference, but try to choose the one that *most* closely describes you.

Worship

❏ 1. I like a carefully planned worship service in the same order every Sunday.

❏ 2. I am moved by a spontaneous worship time, where people's feelings come to the forefront.

❏ 3. Worship should be simple, with times of silence built in for reflection.

❏ 4. I worship God by my acts of service, not by what I do inside a building.

Time

❏ 1. Worship should begin promptly at 10:30 and end at 11:30.

❏ 2. If the Spirit is moving in the service, the length of the worship shouldn't make a difference.

❏ 3. All time is God's time.

❏ 4. We should come together for worship whenever and however long as needed.

Prayer

❏ 1. Prayer should be lofty and poetic, with special words that ask for knowledge and God's guidance.

❏ 2. Prayer doesn't have to use special language and should reflect the feelings of the people talking to God.

❏ 3. Prayer should be a time of silence, being in God's presence and listening for God's voice.

❏ 4. How I live and what I do are my prayer to God.

Music

❏ 1. The music should be lofty and inspirational, praising God in melody and words.

❏ 2. The music should reflect the congregation, uniting the group in an act of community praise.

❏ 3. Music should be that which calms the soul and opens the person to the presence of God, a chant or a tonal sound.

❏ 4. Music should be inspirational and motivating the people to do great things for God.

Preaching

❏ 1. An excellently and rightly preached sermon is the most important part of worship.

❏ 2. The Gospel is preached effectively so that when people leave their lives are changed.

❏ 3. When the heart is moved, however it happens, then the Spirit of God has been heard.

❏ 4. Our lives are a sermon and how we live them speaks louder than any words a pastor can utter.

Emphasis

❏ 1. It is important to me that I find my calling and how God wants me to live out this calling in the world.

❏ 2. It is important to me to live a holy life and to live in a loving relationship with God.

❏ 3. It is important to me to feel as though I am one with God.

❏ 4. It is important to me to live out what God calls me to be and do by.preaching to others.

Support of Causes

❏ 1. I think it is important to support our seminaries, our publishing house, scholarships for students, and preaching to others.

❏ 2. I think we should support evangelism, missions, and by taking the Word to the masses.

❏ 3. I think we should support retreat centers, spiritual directions, and liturgical reform.

❏ 4. I support political action to establish justice in society and its institutions.

Totals

Total your numbers:

_____ 1s

_____ 2s

_____ 3s

_____ 4s

If you have:

More 1s: look at the description for Head Spirituality.

More 2s: Look at the description for Heart Spirituality.

More 3s: Look at the description for Mystic Spirituality.

More 4s: Look at the description for Kingdom Spirituality.

Head Spirituality

You tend to be a person whose spirituality is a "thinking" or Head spirituality. You tend to favor what you can see, touch, or imagine. Order is very important to you. You seek that which will help you live out your vocation in the world. You enjoy theological discussions as long as they stick to the "facts." You belong to the group of people who made sure that the Scriptures were written down, codified, and passed on from generation to generation.

Heart Spirituality

Your spirituality is more of a "feeling" or Heart spirituality. You have combined the feeling world with the real-life world which works very well for you. You seek personal transformation from your church experience. You belong to the group of people for which the immanence of God is more important than the transcendence of God. God is real and here now. Personal service is important but only if it allows you to witness to your faith. Witness and proclamation are important and you are willing to use the tools of technology to accomplish your goals.

Mystic Spirituality

You find your spirituality in the realm of the spirit or Mystic spirituality. God is unnameable and more vast than any one person can ever know. People who find themselves in this category tend to be more introspective and contemplative in their faith. God's response to Moses, "I AM WHO I AM!" makes perfect sense to a person who leans toward this realm. Your goal is to simplify your life so that you can be more tuned in to the inner voice of God.

Kingdom Spirituality

If you are a Kingdom Spiritualist, you are part of a very hard-to-identify group, mainly because these persons are rarely found within the walls of a church to be counted. You are most likely a political activist and have little patience with those who are not. You tend to be aggressive in trying to bring about the Kingdom of God. Prayer, worship, and theology are all equated, at least in your domain, with action. The vision goes before you, and you drive forward with enthusiasm.

Because of limited space, we can only identify the different spiritual types here and provide some insight into their main characteristics. We encourage persons to experience other worship types and to acknowledge their gifts. For more in-depth information read *Discover Your Spiritual Type: A Guide to Individual and Congregational Growth,* by Corinne Ware (an Alban Institute Publication, 1995).

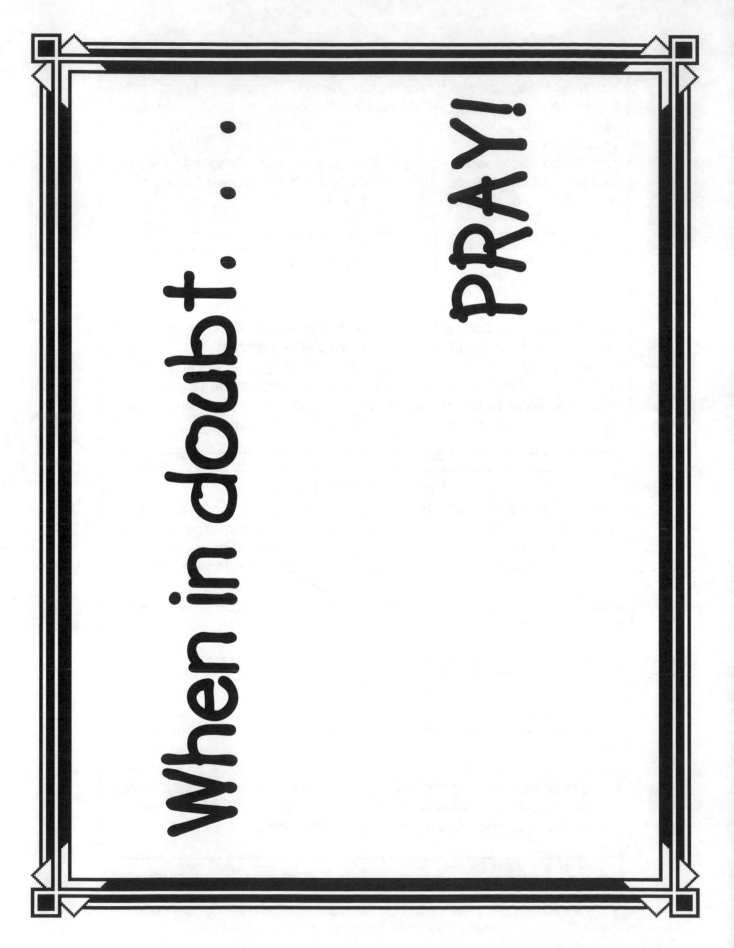

When in doubt. . . .

PRAY!

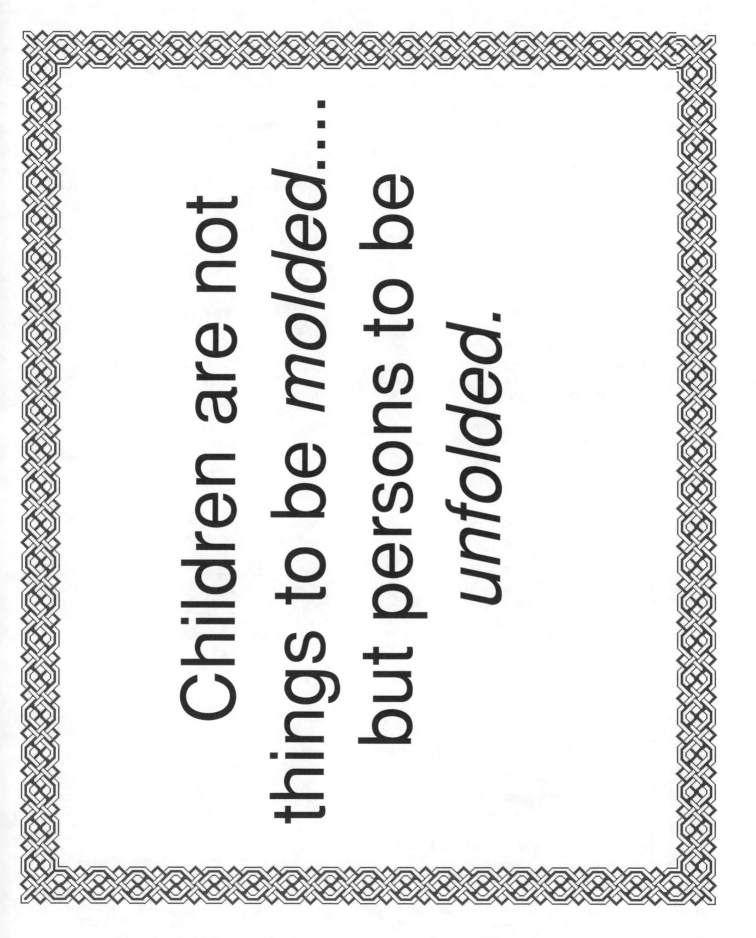

Children are not things to be be *molded*... but persons to be *unfolded.*

Age-Level Knowledge and

Ages	Developing Faith Foundations	Knowing Bible and Faith Traditions
Birth to 2	• to have an attractive, safe space that encourages personal development and awareness of others • to have loving, caring adults who help them experience trust • to be guided in respecting others' rights and in being friends • to have basic love expressed through gentleness blended with sufficient firmness.	• to recognize the Bible as a special book with special significance • to associate the name 'Jesus' with pictures and with the Bible • to hear Bible stories and to be shown where those stories are located in the Bible.
Ages 3-5	• to be with adults with Christian attitudes and behaviors that children can imitate • to have their feelings and actions accepted and to be forgiven when they do not meet adult expectations • to be guided in playing cooperatively with other children without fighting • to practice decision-making through optional activities.	• to handle the Bible and see others read from it • to sing and say Bible verses, especially from the Psalms and Gospels • to recognize the Lord's Prayer, Doxology, and other commonly used aspects of our faith tradition • to hear stories of Bible people who lived as God wanted them to live • to participate in Communion with parents or other caregivers • to hear short stories about the church today and in the past.
Ages 6-8	• to plan and carry out both group and individual activities • to be guided in dealing with classroom situations in ways that are Christian • to be given responsibility in helping to care for the classroom and class environment • to hear stories about and have experiences with persons who are different from them • to investigate, experiment, and explore.	• to repeat the Lord's Prayer with others • to hear a simple explanation of the sacraments • to read simple verses from the Bible • to hear more detailed stories from the Bible • to know the names of the books of the Bible used most frequently in their class and how to locate them in the Bible • to hear stories of people who have helped the church come to us • to use Bibles at home as well as at church.
Ages 9-12	• to be guided in developing and practicing thinking skills • to develop a sense of belonging to the faith community • to participate in meaningful ways in the worship and the work of the congregation • to share with faith friends of various age levels • to be able to affirm self as a child of God.	• to learn the names of all the books of the Bible • to learn to use age-level-appropriate study tools such as a concordance, atlas, and dictionary • to use and understand creeds and hymns used most frequently in church worship • to know various kinds of writings in the Bible • to explore Bible stories in historical context • to learn about the history and teaching of The United Methodist Church • to increase and use vocabulary related to the Christian faith.

Experiences Children Need

Relating to God and the Church	Relating Faith to Life
• to observe parents and teachers pray, read the Bible, and talk about God and their own faith • to experience trust in others which will later serve as a foundation for trust in God • to offer thanks to God by saying brief prayers and by placing offerings in the collection plate • to experience faith through baptism and the care of the congregation.	• to hear people talk about God, Jesus, and the Bible during the week as well as on Sunday • to see pictures of children's daily experiences in church classrooms • to hear teachers and parents pray for food and other daily needs.
• to learn simple prayers • to be encouraged to give their own offerings to God and the church • to develop a sense of belonging at church and as a child of God • to have accepting adults who are willing to hear their many questions about God, life, death, and crises • to experience awe and wonder through nature, life cycles, and corporate worship even though they may not be able to talk about the meanings of their experiences.	• to hear stories about service to others and to observe teachers, parents, and older children in service to others • to participate in service by making things for others and by sharing money and food • to hear teachers and parents pray about people and situations outside the classroom • to use Sunday school take-home items as reminders during the week • to practice appreciating and caring for God's world.
• to participate in corporate worship • to pray their own prayers in class and at home • to be with adults who are open to children's questions about God even if adults say they don't know the answers • to have the understanding of adults who know children experience more of God than they can express verbally. • to be encouraged to consider the rights of other children and family members	• to participate in service projects appropriate to their age levels and abilities • to relate the joys and concerns of daily living to Bible teachings through visual aids, activities, stories, and discussions • to be reminded that God expects us to love everyone, including our enemies • to learn key Bible verses to think about during the week.
• to be guided in making a commitment to God through Jesus Christ • to have a sense of belonging to both the local church and the larger faith community • to be guided in understanding the meaning of church membership • to verbalize experiences and questions about God and faith, including doubts • to find guidance for disciplines of prayer and Bible reading • to see Christian growth as a lifelong process • to learn the importance of obedience and responsibility in the covenant relationship with God.	• to hear and discuss stories of ways others live out their faith in various circumstances • to be guided and assisted in practicing spiritual discipline • to identify and express attitudes, ideas, and feelings about unfairness, injustice, and social evil • to clarify and develop their senses of right and wrong in light of Christian faith • to serve with others in the community and world • to struggle with moral and ethical issues in the light of Christian faith • to be given concrete suggestions and opportunities for ways to be in discipleship.

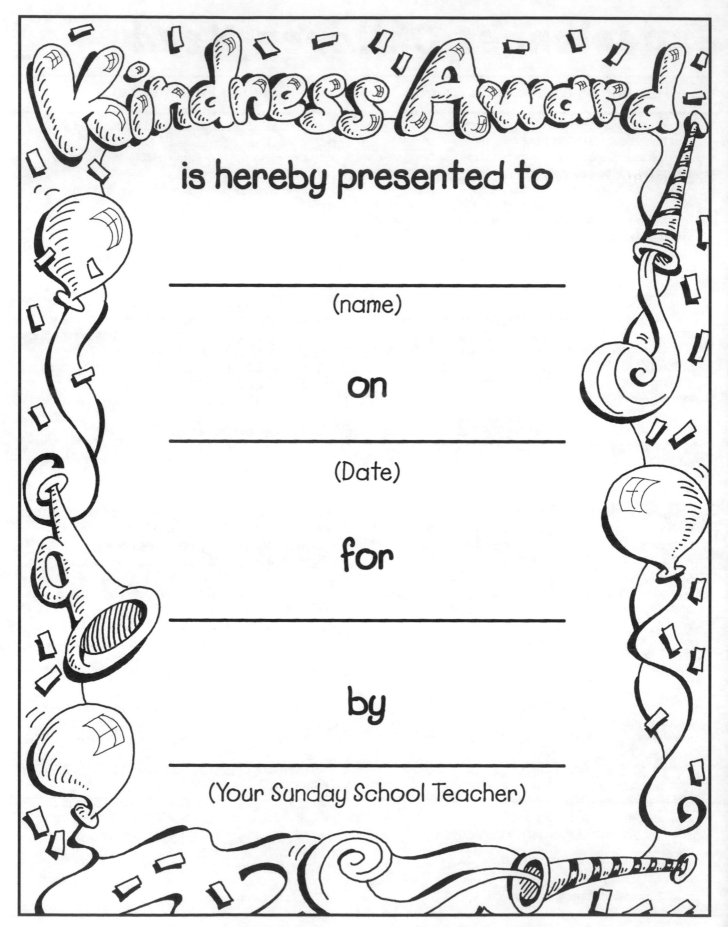

Kindness Award

is hereby presented to

_____

(name)

on

_____

(Date)

for

_____

by

_____

(Your Sunday School Teacher)

Factors That Encourage Learning

Intentionally well-arranged rooms or space

Good ventilation, heating, and cooling

Adequate natural light, good electric lighting, or both

Tables and chairs (or other seating) of proper height and comfort level for the age group

Bulletin board and chalkboards at comfortable eye and work levels

Adequate floor space for easy student and teacher mobility

Enclosed storage space as well as open storage for frequently used materials

Wastebaskets available

Adequate supplies for students (paper, scissors, paste, pencils, leaflets)

A clean rug, drapes, wall, floor

A way to display the children's work (bulletin board, wall space, cork strip, picture rail, clothes-line)

Permanent pictures, if any, appropriate for the age group

Newsprint easel or chalkboard available

Classroom well marked with name or age group

Piano, cassette/CD player available

Display of children's current work in this unit

Normal classroom noise and activity adequately absorbed

Factors That Discourage Learning

Chairs and tables too small or too large for students

Room temperature that cannot be regulated

General student activity that disturbs people and classes nearby

Noise from other people and classes that disturbs students

Room looking disarrayed and neglected

Last year's students' work still on display

Room or space marked with wrong age level or not marked at all

Out-of-season posters and pictures still displayed

Chalkboard and bulletin board out of reach of students

Room used by another group, and class interrupted each week

Supplies and resources not organized

Light too direct

Room with more furniture than is used by class

Inadequate supplies and other resources for each student

No place available for displaying students' work

Cassette/CD player or piano not available or not working properly

Trash and discarded material accumulating on tables and floor

Permanent pictures, if any, not appropriate to the age level

Room furniture limited and providing no way for students to do their work and study

Classroom not inspiring to me, the teacher

42

Teaching All God's Children

Each child in your class is unique. Each one has his or her own unique combination of gender, skin color, size, personality, and interests. But perhaps less obvious is the variety of unique ways used by the students to learn in your class. Let's take a look at learning styles.

Learning style? What's that?

A learning style is the way a person perceives and processes information so that it becomes meaningful.

What's that got to do with teaching?

Every person has a preferred learning style. It is not preferred because the person has chosen it; it is preferred because of developmental factors that have made that way of learning the most effective for that particular person.

Does that mean that each person learns in only one way?

Oh, no! It simply means that each person learns most effectively when material is presented in his or her preferred learning style. But all people can learn in many ways. They learn best, in fact, when they experience many learning styles. But sometimes it takes an experience with the preferred learning style to get someone started.

What if each of my students has a different learning style?

Think variety! Provide activities in your class that involve children with many styles of learning. Be sure that there are some activities that appeal to each child's preferred learning style. Then encourage the students to try out other learning styles. They may learn to enjoy new ways of learning.

But what if they want to do activities that I do not like?

That may happen! Recognize that you too have a preferred learning style. And that's the way you prefer to teach. But the job of a teacher is to structure learning experiences that will enable others to learn. You can experiment with new ways to teach, just as you want your students to experiment with new ways to learn. You will be a better teacher when you expand your own learning and teaching styles.

What are these learning styles?

Learning styles have been described in many ways. Various ways of learning have been grouped into categories and have been given many names over the years. The names are not especially important. What is important, though, is that you as a teacher recognize the varieties of ways your students learn so that you can be the best teacher possible.

These Seven Ways of Knowing Are

1. Verbal
2. Logical
3. Visual
4. Physical
5. Musical
6. Social
7. Independent

Those are big words! Tell me what I need to do to use them.

Sure! Just check out the descriptions and the suggested activities for each of the learning styles on the chart. Then use the planning and observation charts on pages 44–45 to help you plan for teaching using your knowledge of these learning styles. Remember that these ways of knowing (or learning) are interconnected. Each person has a preferred way of learning, but the best learning takes place when we experience it in a variety of ways. The best teaching happens when we use those methods that provide opportunities for learning in many ways!

Type of Learner	Verbal Learner	Logical Learner	Visual Learner
Enjoys	**Words** reading, writing, and talking	**Numbers,** abstract and scientific thinking, reasoning, categories and patterns	**Visualizing** and creating mental images, manipulating shapes and objects
Learns Best By	Saying things aloud, hearing words spoken, seeing words in print	Asking and answering questions, categorizing and classifying things	Looking at pictures, visualizing and dreaming about concepts and ideas, doodling and drawing
Favorite Activities	• Reading, writing, and telling stories • Writing poems and litanies • Completing sentences • Memorizing names, dates, Bible verses, and trivia • Keeping a journal • Learning new words • Answering questions • Discussing • Playing word games	• Solving number and word puzzles • Conducting experiments • Working with numbers and math • Solving problems • Exploring patterns and relationships • Following step-by-step explanations	• Drawing and art activities • Designing and building models • Watching videos • Following mazes • Using maps, charts, posters, and diagrams • Learning about symbols • Putting together puzzles
Least Favorite Activities	Becomes frustrated without verbal stimulation	Finds it difficult to function in arenas of confusion	Is discouraged by too much printed (*text*) material

Physical Learner	Musical Learner	Social Learner	Independent Learner
Physical movement and active processes	**Music,** songs, and rhythmic patterns	**Social activities,** relationships, communication with others, and working cooperatively in teams	**Thinking** about personal feelings and values, self-reflection, and working independently
Moving while learning; touching objects to be learned about	Using rhythm, melody, and music combined with information	Talking and working with groups, comparing ideas and concepts	Working alone on projects
• Physical activities • Crafts • Motions with songs, stories, and prayers • Touching objects • Dancing • Marching and waving streamers • Role-playing and drama • Pantomime • Fingerplays • Active games	• Singing, humming, listening to music • Writing songs • Making and playing musical instruments • Learning Bible verses set to music • Listening to and learning story songs • Rapping • Writing new words to familiar tunes • Learning hymns • Rhythm games • Listening to sounds	• Interviews • Discussion and dialogue • Asking and answering questions • Cooperative learning games • Working together in small groups • Parties and celebrations • Service projects	• Focusing on inner feelings • Identifying with characters in a story • Research projects • Prayer and meditation • Journaling
Is turned off by inactivity—sitting for long periods of time.	Is bored by lectures.	Is stifled by long periods of silent study.	May withdraw from group activities.

Exercise Six:
Observing Your Children

Write the names of the children in your class down the side of the chart. Observe the ways the children in your class respond to each of the activities you plan for them over a period of several weeks. When you notice that a child seems to enjoy a particular activity, make a check mark beside that child's name under the description of the type of activity. Some boxes on the chart may be filled with many check marks after several weeks of observation. Other boxes may have only one mark or even none.

Study your chart after a few weeks. What can you learn about your children's learning methods? What do the marks suggest about your plans for teaching in the future?

- Are there some activities that most of the children enjoy?
- Are there some activities that no one responds to very well?

- Is there a child who doesn't seem to enjoy *anything* you plan?
- Are there some types of learning activities that you have never used?
- Is there a child who responds to only one type of activity?
- Are there some children who seem to enjoy almost anything you plan?
- What does the chart suggest about changes you might make in planning for teaching?

Remember: You *do not* want to simply plan more activities that you know the children will enjoy. You want to find ways to get children involved in a *variety* of learning styles. Create an atmosphere that also encourages learning in new ways.

Child's Name	Verbal	Logical	Visual	Physical	Musical	Social	Independent	Child's Name	Verbal	Logical	Visual	Physical	Musical	Social	Independent

OUT OF THE BOX

Exercise Seven:
Evaluate Your Teaching Style

Keep a record of the teaching styles you choose as you plan the class time for your children over a period of several weeks. As you plan, write the date the lesson will be taught. Then make a check mark on the chart to show the learning styles that you will make available for the children in that lesson.

Study your chart after a few weeks. What do the check marks reveal about your own learning and teaching styles?

- Are there more check marks under some learning and teaching styles at the bottom of the chart than there were at the beginning?
- Have you consciously planned activities you might have overlooked if you were not thinking about adding variety to the ways you and your children learn?
- Have you discovered any new ways to teach and learn that you appreciate more than you thought you would?
- Have you noticed any change in the ways children respond to the kinds of activities you plan?
- What do the marks say to you about how you will plan each week's lesson in the future?

Remember: The many ways of learning are interconnected. The best teaching happens when you plan opportunities for learning in many ways. Experiment! Learn some new ways to teach and help your children discover some new ways to learn. In doing so you will be a better teacher, and your students will be better learners.

Date Lesson Will Be Taught	Verbal	Logical	Visual	Physical	Musical	Social	Independent	Date Lesson Will Be Taught	Verbal	Logical	Visual	Physical	Musical	Social	Independent	Date Lesson Will Be Taught	Verbal	Logical	Visual	Physical	Musical	Social	Independent

USING LEARNING CENTERS

What are learning centers?

Learning centers consist of ways of organizing and presenting material to children that make it possible to incorporate the children's different learning styles.

Learning centers extend the learning experience, encouraging children to pursue this topic beyond the activities provided in the Sunday school setting.

Why use learning centers?

- Learning centers offer children choices of activities.
- Learning centers provide active discovery opportunities.
- Learning centers cut down on the boredom factor.
- Learning centers offer the children opportunities to share and talk with other children as they explore and learn.
- Learning centers affirm each child as a child of God with unique skills and abilities.
- Learning centers are fun!

What are the different kinds of learning centers?

Programmed Centers:
These start with a conversation time for all students. Then each child will plan his or her own schedule.

Open Centers:
Each child is free to move from one center to another center on her or his own. You will assist children in making center selections.

Small Group Rotation:
Children are grouped into teams of three or four members (*or larger for full-room learning centers*). Each group works at a center task together. At a determined signal by the teacher, each group will rotate to the next center task.

Multi-Station Centers:
The children are involved in a wide variety of activities set up in the room for a short period of time (*three to five minutes, for example*). The activities will consist of a number of different tasks the participants rotate to and from at a specified time.

Enrichment Centers:
Children move from center to center after a pre-arranged group time (after the Bible story time, for example) or work time.

How do I arrange the room?

Room arrangement is not as complicated as it may seem. Once you push all the tables and chairs back out of the way, you can get a better feel for your available space. Even small rooms can effectively have learning centers as long as you look at the space creatively. Floor space becomes just as important as table space. Try partitioning off a corner with a screen, a bookcase, or a piano back to create an activity area. Look around your house, garage, variety stores, discount centers, or garage sales for things that will make your room look comfortable and functional.

How do I start a learning center experience?

All children need structure. They need to know what the routine of the day will be. Centers are not "free-for-alls." Centers require organization and planning in order to be successful. Teachers who are just beginning to use centers may start small and add an enrichment center each week. Set up the ground rules for use of the center, including how many persons can be at the center at one time and how long they can be there. Getting too much material too soon can be very confusing for the children.

Consider these questions:
1. Do the children know how to use all the materials at the center?
2. Do the children know where to put their projects when they are finished?
3. Does the center need adult supervision?
4. Are there children who will need special assistance?
5. Is space a factor? How many children can be at any center at one time?
6. How will I know if the children are learning anything?

Suggested Schedule

Greeting/Welcoming Time (*as children arrive*)	Welcome the children individually.
Arrival Activities (*5 to 10 minutes*)	Easily finished activities that will involve the children and introduce concepts of the Bible message
Group Time (*10 to 15 minutes*)	Conversation time, Bible reading, Bible story time
Learning Centers (*20 to 30 minutes*)	Activities that allow the children to apply the Bible message, practice Bible skills, engage in creative expression, and explore ideas
Cleanup (*2 to 3 minutes*)	Encourage children to clean up the area. Make this an enjoyable experience.
Closing Worship (*8 to 10 minutes*)	Bring the children back together; share any learnings from center time; recall the main ideas; share in active music; and close with worship.

What are the secrets to successful learning centers?

Keep the centers fresh:
Change activities in the centers frequently enough to keep the children's interest. As interest wanes in the activities of a center, add new activities to the center. Good planning makes good learning centers.

Introduce new activities slowly:
Too many new games and tasks can be confusing, especially if they include new learnings. Games with lots of rules should be introduced to the class as a whole instead of only a few children at one time. Playing a game with a few children as they come into the room will allow children to teach one another at a later time.

Decide what your role as teacher will be:
Learning centers are fun, but they are just that— "learning" centers. Emphasize the work the children will be accomplishing at each center. Will you be an **observer,** assisting only as the children need you? Will you be the **ringmaster,** directing the activities for the time allotted? Will you be the **tour guide,** helping children decide what to do next and advising them on activities that will appeal to them?

Control the Noise Ahead of Time:
Learning centers by their nature are a bit noisier than the traditional class sessions. How much noise is allowable is at the teacher's discretion (*and that of the other classes close by*). Ask yourself if the noise is busy and productive or just noise. Remind the children of the standards and atmosphere you require. Remind children to "talk only loudly enough for the friend next to you to hear you."

A Pat on the Back Is Always Good:

Children like to know they are doing a good job. If you see a child working particularly hard at a task, lending a hand to a friend, or even straightening up the center nicely after use, let the child (and the class) know about it. Share these contributions at the closing class time. Reward the children with special stickers, a Happygram, or a Good Work Ribbon.

Share the Learnings:

Provide a time for the children to share their experiences of the day. It will be surprising how many learning experiences may have taken place that you did not even expect. Invite the children to evaluate the centers and identify any particular problems they may have encountered. Ask for suggestions for improvement.

Keep Track:

Many teachers want to know where each child is currently working. A large chart is a convenient way to see where each child is working on any particular day. Write a child's name on a clothespin and let the child move the clothespin from center to center. This is also a good way to limit the number of children involved at one center at a given time. Use a rainbow color coding system and let the children color spaces that represent the centers they visit, if you want to make sure that they visit all the centers. Before a child can repeat a center, he or she must have completed all the centers.

Parents Can Be Lifesavers:

Assisting at a center is a good way to involve parents in the learning environment without a great deal of time commitment. Send out a cry for "help" in the fall, and then schedule your volunteers so that they have good experiences but don't get overworked. Sit down and make a list of exactly what you want the volunteers to do before you elicit their help. Parents might even be willing to help you set up centers by creating the "visuals" at home.

Choosing Your Resources

Teaching children about the faith is probably one of the most important ministries of the church. Teachers depend upon the curriculum they choose to make this ministry exciting, theologically sound, and educationally appropriate for their situation. So how do you choose the right curriculum for your church?

Sunday school leaders today are flooded with brochures and samples of Sunday school materials that promise to be easy to use, offer better learning experiences, and that claim to enable a teacher to teach in the best possible way. More than half of the new members in many churches today come from other denominations. Because children often come from different backgrounds, with different traditions, and different expectations, the choice of Sunday school curriculum needs to be regularly questioned. With so many choices and so many promises, how does a church evaluate and make the best choice for the education program? People of faith always seek God's guidance, even in the midst of lists, goals, and exercises. Being in a spirit and attitude of prayer will help your Sunday school leaders in discerning the best materials to reach your church's Christian education goals.

One Church's Experience

One congregation in a community had several children's classes. Everyone in the group had been using the same curriculum until the year this story took place. But two of the new teachers had used another curriculum in their previous church. They had been pleased with the ease of teaching and how little preparation was required. Surely, this curriculum could be used in their new congregation. It had a proven track record in their other congregation, so the two new teachers went to see the director of education at their church and explained their desires.

The director had heard of this other curriculum but was not very familiar with it. The director wanted all the children's classes to be using the same material. Besides, the curriculum they currently were using was the approved denominational curriculum. Change was not something to be undertaken frivolously or quickly. Some serious study had to be done. The director didn't want to dismiss the idea offhand without a look at the new curriculum. If this other curriculum was so good and easy to use, might they not want to use it across all age levels?

The director of education called all the teachers together on a Sunday afternoon. The first thing they did was talk about what they expected curriculum to do. Then they made a list of "must have" criteria for the curriculum. The very first thing on the list was that the Bible had to be dominant in each lesson. The second thing on the list was that the material had to be theologically in line with their denomination. And so the list grew with the criteria the teachers felt was important.

Armed with this information and a checklist of specifics, the director gave each teacher samples of the age level of the new curriculum to compare to the curriculum they were currently using. They agreed to meet on the following Sunday and bring in their findings.

At the end of the second meeting the teachers shared their findings and at the end voted to stay with their denominational resources. The new curriculum did offer some pluses for the teacher and a few for the children, but overall it did not measure up to what they had decided a good Sunday school curriculum to do.

Listed below are the criteria they used:

Biblical Integrity
- Is the Bible treated with respect and authority?
- Are the stories consistent with Scripture?
- Is the art biblically accurate?

Scope and Sequence
- Are both the Old and New Testaments of the Bible taught?
- Is there a heavy concentration on one or the other?
- What Bible stories will be taught and in what order?
- Is the material appropriate for the age level?
- Are all the appropriate parts of Scripture taught, or just a few areas?
- Does the material offer expanded materials and faith concepts as the children grow older?

Theological Integrity and Compatibility
- What is the view held by the resources on God, Jesus, the Bible, humanity, sin, grace, and forgiveness?
- Are these views compatible with those of our congregation?

Inclusiveness
- Are persons of color of equal importance to Caucasians in stories and activities?
- Are inclusive stories and activities authentic?
- Are there gender stereotypes?
- Are persons with disabilities shown in ministry rather than being only ministered to?

Teaching Styles
- Are there a variety of activities in each lesson?
- Does the material encompass all the seven learning styles at some time during the quarter?
- Are children offered choices?
- Are the activities creative and do they allow the children to express their own personal feelings?
- Is the material compatible with your denomination's doctrine and beliefs?

Choosing What is Taught
- What is explicitly taught in each lesson?
- What is taught implicitly in each lesson?
- What is intentionally left out?

Adapted from *What You See Is What You Get*, by Gerald Chambers.
© 2000 Cokesbury.

Shared Space: It's a Matter of Discipleship

by Richard Whitaker

"Why don't those Sunday school teachers ever put the toys back in the right place?" "We don't even have a bulletin board to put our curriculum art prints on; they're so greedy!" "Those day care people—they think they own this building!"

If this situation sounds all too familiar you are among the many Sunday school, nursery school, day care, and youth ministry workers who share space in classrooms and fellowship halls.

Begin at the Beginning

Why does your church exist? Does it have a mission statement or statement of purpose? If it does, that statement probably includes phrases like "offering the love of Jesus Christ to all people through opportunities for service, and equipping them for discipleship." It will be easy from such a statement to see that those opportunities will come in many varieties, most offered within the limitations of your facility.

Make Room for Everyone

So who has first claim on the church building? If *everything* your church does falls within the mission statement, *everything* is first priority! Ministries held on Sunday are not more important than ministries held during the week. And ministries to "our people" (church members and friends) are not more important than ministries to and with "the outsiders" (day care families), because all are ministries of the church. Once ministries are adopted by the administrative council or board they become ministries of the whole church.

Consider the Opportunities

Consider the opportunities that shared space affords all persons, rather than bickering and creating a mentality of "us" and "them." With shared space we can
• view ourselves and the programs we offer as partners in ministry, benefitting all persons;
• see the advantages of having more toys or equipment. Often, one group alone cannot afford to provide these:

- recognize the wise stewardship of having rooms used five to six days a week rather than only one day a week;
- practice cooperation and compromise among groups;
- live out God's requirement to love our neighbors and practice hospitality.

The larger a church, the more diverse its ministry and programs are, and the more careful planning, coordination, and conflict resolution is needed. Here are some practical suggestions:

Plan for Success

1. Be aware of recommended floor space needs for the ratios (according to age) of children and adults, as determined by your state's childcare licensing standards. Consider the kinds of activities (movement, seated study, learning centers, small groups). Analyze average weekly attendance figures for Sunday school or youth groups when planning which groups might share common rooms.

2. Consider the size and types of furnishings and equipment in the room. Obviously, you would not house a four-year-old weekday nursery school in the same space with a fifth-sixth grade Sunday school class.

3. Label cabinets and shelves for ease in locating, retrieving, and returning art supplies, toys, and audiovisual equipment. To aid the nonreaders, use pictures of toys glued or taped to shelves, rather than names

of toys. Expensive or specific age-appropriate equipment and toys purchased and used by one group only are usually best kept in secured cabinets. These can remain separate from other puzzles, toys, dress-up clothes, and musical instruments left out in the open and accessible.

4. Purchase and store food items. Sunday school teachers, youth groups, and occasional users would be served well by having their own small refrigerators and food storage areas. The practical reasons for this often have to do with allergies and special foods brought by weekday children, milk subsidies for day care purchases, and the shelf life of perishable foods used daily, as opposed to weekly.

5. Install and assign adequate numbers of bulletin boards or tack strips to each classroom. At least one display area should be assigned for every separate group using the shared space. Keep in mind that art prints from the curriculum class packs enhance the learning environment for weekday children and staff and serve to remind everyone of the Christian environment in which we all labor and learn.

6. Determine custodial services. Will weekday areas be cleaned by church custodians, or are other part-time custodians needed? What are the basic housekeeping tasks that all should assume in consideration for others?

Get Coordinated!

1. Determine who makes decisions about space and equipment. Often a staff Christian educator, pastor, or volunteer chairperson of the education work area is duly authorized to make recommendations to the administrative board or church council. Such recommendations should be thoroughly discussed in advance with the church's day care or nursery school director and any other ministry groups or outside "tenant" user groups who will be using space.

2. Develop a written shared space policy that can be agreed upon and signed by designated representatives of all groups. Include those affirmative statements and specifics in such a policy as previously listed.

3. Establish a clear process for handling problems or grievances when they occur.

4. Distribute the approved written policy. Be sure all weekday staff, Sunday school staff, and youth personnel know what is expected and how to build bridges of harmony rather than resentment. Each class should have the names and phone numbers of others sharing their room from week to week, along with the agreed-upon room policy.

5. Coordinate ministry goals and objectives and how shared space can enhance those desired outcomes. Two examples follow,
a. Identify a storage area that can be cleaned, redesigned, and developed into a teacher resource center that all teachers would use. Such a center might include extra games, puzzles, how-to teacher hints or Bible reference books, recycled music cassettes, art prints, and items neither easily stored nor regularly needed in the classroom.
b. Begin a weekly chapel class using the chapel or library as a place for Christian storytelling, music, and prayer with weekday children and staff members.
Both of these suggestions can go a long way in educating the "whole" child and in nurturing the teacher as well.

Resolve Conflict

1. Accept the reality that problems do occur. The key to minimizing "us" and "them" talk is to stay in communication. Fewer feelings are hurt when all groups sharing space have a designated liaison to whom problems may be addressed. It is both unhealthy and counterproductive for volunteers or paid weekday staff to leave notes for one another accusing one another of violating or misusing space.

2. Don't allow problems to fester over time. Talk out the problems as they occur. Be willing to renegotiate space as situations change (such as when a before- or after-school care program begins or expands).

3. Update written policies, and be sure all new volunteers and weekday staff receive these policies as they begin their service.

4. Call in a mediator when emotions run high and your best efforts are at an impasse.

5. Recognize and use the power of prayer in seeking solutions to space problems.

Rewards Outweigh Problems

We overcome the battles of "us" and "them" when we understand our task from the perspective that we are all God's children. We live, learn, work together, and joyfully share space as God intends.

———

Richard Whitaker, Diaconal Minister of Christian Education at Whitefish Bay UMC (Wisconsin), has written curriculum and many articles for Church Educator magazine and the Children's Fund for Christian Mission packet.

From Children's Teacher, Vol. 7, No. 1. © 1999 Cokesbury

The Ca, ing Teache,

Caring is important in teaching and learning because learning is enhanced when children are surrounded by love, warmth, acceptance, and compassion.

When over a thousand people were asked what they valued in their Sunday school teacher, the phrase "loves and is concerned about people" was at the top of the list, and included in the top eight items was the phrase "personally knows those in his or her group."

The teacher creates a climate of caring for the whole class. This caring climate includes listening, including new persons in the group, embracing the one or two people who always seem to move, or are pushed, to the edges of the group, and preparing for the awesome task of teaching that which transforms people into the image of Christ.

Some specific caring actions a teacher might take:

- Pray for each child in the group and for a vital teaching and learning experience.
- Become acquainted with each child's home life. Remember that today many families do not fit the traditional concept of a nuclear family with mother, father, and children.
- Invite, and urge members of the group to invite, new children to the group. Offer or secure a ride for them. Many children do not attend church because they are never asked. Encourage the children to seek out others.
- Help the children become acquainted with one another. Make the classroom a place where hospitality is practiced, where the children are included, and where the contributions they make are accepted.
- Provide a clean, attractive, and safe space.
- Discover the interests and concerns of the children.
- Prepare for the teaching and learning experience with specific children in mind.
- Explore ways to involve the children in your class.

- Make sure that discussion sessions do not always consist of the same children's contributions. Use language that includes all persons.
- Take seriously children's questions and ideas.
- Make sure your session helps the children explore the application of new learnings to daily life.
- Remember that touch—an appropriate touch—is important for both children and persons of all ages.
- Visit, call, or write a note to children who miss sessions, especially several sessions.

Helping children make connections between the story of God's grace as experienced in Jesus Christ and their own personal stories is a vital, caring act. The teaching task is not only about the transmission of information about the Bible, beliefs, and moral values of the church. The teaching task is also about making connections between that information and a child's life. Teachers care about experiences in ways that are appropriate to the group they lead.

Adapted from *Caring That Transforms* © 2000 Cokesbury

Explore God's Creation

"Just What Can a Teacher Do?"

by Elizabeth Crocker

"She messed up my picture!"
"This is a dumb story!"

Chances are that remarks like these do not come to mind when you think of Sunday school. Like most of us, you probably picture a happy classroom full of children experiencing God's love and God's word. Indeed, that happy class is our goal as Sunday school teachers! However, reaching this goal usually requires some skillful and creative behavior management.

What Is the Range of Normal Behavior? Recognizing that it is normal for children to exhibit occasional negative, oppositional, and even aggressive behavior is the first step toward viewing these problem behaviors as opportunities rather than roadblocks. Children may experience forgiveness and grace, depending on our response. They may practice discipleship through acts of kindness and reconciliation. Part of a child's faith journey is the development of self-discipline, which is the goal of good behavior management practices in the classroom. Here are some good practices for all age levels.

Know your children. Know about the kinds of developmental tasks that are common to all children at the ages of your students. But don't stop there; know your children personally too. Call them by name. Know about their families, interests, and experiences during the week. This knowledge will provide insights

about behavior patterns and motivation while showing interest in the children. Your relationship with the children must be nurtured—it is in the context of this relationship that you represent Jesus Christ.

Plan lessons carefully. A well-planned lesson is the single best deterrent to problem behaviors, though it may not prevent them entirely. Be sure to have enough lessons planned so that children are engaged in a learning activity the moment they enter the room. (Learning centers are great for this purpose!) Provide a variety of activities that are alternately active and calm, loud and quiet, group and individual.

Design the space to fit the children.
Use anything from boxes to bookshelves. Create interest areas within the room to break up the space and encourage purposeful activity. Include a place such as a story rug for gathering the class together. Be sure that you can see the children wherever they are in the room.

Make expectations clear. Children need to know what the rules are and that you expect them to behave appropriately. Remember that children respond to your tone of voice, body language, and other nonverbal cues. Be sure to send a clear message that communicates your love and respect along with your expectations. Let the children know that you believe they are able to make good choices and praise them when they do this.

Reinforce good behavior. Tangible reinforcements for good behavior may be helpful, particularly with large groups. When a preschool child shares a toy, he or she may be invited to add a paper link to a friendship chain that is displayed in the classroom, for example. Elementary children may enjoy adding pieces to a picture puzzle that ties into the unit theme. Or, they may enjoy collecting letters that spell a key unit word or phrase like A-M-B-A-S-S-A-D-O-R-S F-O-R C-H-R-I-S-T. You may wish to celebrate as a class upon completion of your chosen activity. Be

sure to use such methods to *reinforce* good behavior, not to manipulate.

Model respect but claim authority.
Respect and authority are vague notions for some children, and these concepts are frequently ridiculed in popular television shows. However, they are central to our faith, especially to the experience of worship and the understanding of Jesus as Lord. Treat the children with respect by using kind words and actions, and expect them to do likewise. Tell the children what you will do if misbehavior occurs. Use redirection, reminders, restitution, and removal from the immediate situation (such as a thinking chair) as needed. Do so consistently and without ridicule. However, be careful not to overuse the thinking chair and other time-out measures. Keep time-out periods brief and directed toward helping the child examine her or his response to the situation. Meanwhile, keep the class focused on the lesson and continue with activities as planned.

Redirect behavior early. Shift the child's focus to another activity or conversation before trouble starts. Often this early intervention prevents problem behavior and provides children with coping strategies as well.

Involve parents in positive ways. Send home "happygrams" that tell parents one specific positive behavior demonstrated by their child or children. It will be much easier to approach parent(s) about problem behaviors if you reinforce their children's positive behaviors regularly with them. When problem behaviors occur, approach the parent(s) by asking for help. Be as specific as possible, and be sure to express your concern both for the child and for the needs of your class. Maintain contact with the parent(s) if problems persist, and enlist the help of your Sunday school superintendent, age-level coordinator, Christian educator, or pastor.

Correct; don't condemn. When misbehavior occurs, a gentle reminder may be all that is needed to correct it. Elementary children may benefit from a reminder in the form of a question, such as "I've been thinking about God's Golden Rule, about treating others the way you would like to be treated. How could we do that in this situation?" Avoid telling children such things as "Jesus is watching." Instead, affirm Christlike choices as acts of faith and discipleship, especially with older elementary children.

Offer choices when real choices exist. Appropriate choices allow children to feel a sense of control over their actions, a necessary component of self-discipline. Some situations may not warrant choices, and this is okay. Children need to know that some things are not negotiable. You may allow children to choose to read the Bible story by reading aloud and taking turns, reading silently, or by listening to an audiotape, for example. However, everyone will be expected to be involved in reading the Bible story; other activities will be put aside.

Acknowledge feelings. This acknowledgment helps children understand themselves while experiencing your concern for them. An example of this is to tell a child "Sally, I can see that you are frustrated because Bobby is sitting in the chair you wanted, but I cannot allow you to push Bobby. You will need to tell him that you are sorry, and we will think together about another way to solve the problem."

Link behavior to consequences. Many children today spend hours watching television programs in which the consequences of behavior are glossed over or omitted altogether. You should not assume that children will make the connection between behavior and consequences on their own. Be intentional about naming behaviors and noting consequences. You could say "I really like

the way you complimented Jamie on his idea. Comments like that make us feel good about ourselves and free to share our ideas" to reinforce the connection between behavior and consequences.

Finally, remember to pray for the children. The task of growing up in this day and age is more daunting than ever, and children need our prayers to survive and thrive as members of the household of faith. The discipline of prayer reminds us that we are not alone; we are partners with God in ministry to children.

———

Elizabeth Crocker lives with her husband and two children in Lugoff, South Carolina, where she teaches school. She is a member of Lyttleton Street United Methodist Church.

From *Children's Teacher*, Vol. 7, No. 1. © 1999 Cokesbury

Supplies of Great Importance

Paper
- newsprint (*18- by 24-inch* size)
- construction paper (*various colors*)
- drawing paper
- writing paper (*appropriate for age level*)
- butcher paper
- brown wrapping paper
- art tissue (*various colors*)
- aluminum foil
- wax paper
- crepe paper
- wallpaper
- paper towels
- recycled newspaper

Paint
- liquid tempera paint
- powdered tempera paint
- acrylic poster paints
- water color paints

Glue
- white glue (*bought in large quantities*)
- glue sticks
- glitter glue

Tape
- masking tape
- clear cellophane tape
- cloth/vinyl tape
- duct tape

Brushes
- wide, flat easel brushes
- small water color brushes
- glue brushes

Scissors
- safety scissors for young children (*including some for left-handers*)
- school scissors for older children
- sewing scissors (*teacher only*)
- pinking shears (*option*)

Writing Utensils
- pencils (*fat and skinny*)
- crayons
- felt-tip markers (*water-based*)
- felt-tip markers (*permanent*)
- colored pencils
- chalk (*colored and plain*)

Miscellaneous Stuff
- yarn (*various colors and weights*)
- string
- ribbon
- modeling clay (*non drying*)
- modeling clay (*air drying*)
- paper clips
- rubber bands
- envelopes (*all sizes*)
- glitter
- garbage bags (*all sizes*)
- grocery bags (*paper and plastic*)
- drinking straws
- index cards (*all sizes*)
- scarfs/blindfolds
- cotton swabs, cotton balls

Absolutely Essential Equipment
- cassette or CD player
- stapler, staples
- paper punch
- pencil sharpener
- crayon sharpener
- large trashcans
- plastic dishpans
- containers for crayons and markers

OUT OF THE BOX

Be a Collector!

Send this list of supplies home with the children at the beginning of each quarter, highlighting any items in particular that you will be needing. Invite a parent who does not wish to teach to help organize the storeroom so that these supplies can be easily retrieved when needed.

acorns
berry baskets
plastic bottle caps
buttons, beads, or broken jewelry
cardboard
cardboard tubes
clothespins
coffee cans
corks
margarine tubs
potato chip cans
empty boxes of all sizes
frozen juice cans
grocery bags
magazines
fabric scraps
newspapers
old shirts
old toothbrushes
disposable aluminum baking pans

pine cones
plastic lids
seeds
shells
shoeboxes
spice jars or baby food jars
squeeze bottles
spools
foam egg cartons
cardboard egg cartons
quart and half-gallon paper cartons
one- and two-liter plastic soda bottles
wallpaper sample books
wood scraps
clean yogurt containers
plastic water bottles
net potato and orange bags
appliance cartons

Permission is granted to photocopy for local church use. © 2001 Abingdon Press.

Where Do I Get It?

Appliance Stores
(large cardboard boxes, appliance cartons)

Computer Store
(paper, large boxes, packing foam)

Contractor
(blueprint paper, scraps of wood)

Dry Cleaners
(shirt cardboard)

Ice Cream Store
(large round cartons)

Newspaper Company
(paper roll ends)

Printing Company
(scrap paper)

Telephone Company
(colored wire, wooden spools)

Textile Company
(fabric scraps, trims, buttons, spools)

Home Improvement Stores
(wallpaper books, tiles, scraps of linoleum, carpet squares, wood scraps, flower pots)

Wood or Lumber Mill
(sawdust, wood scraps, sandpaper)

DIFFERENT BIBLE STUDIES FOR DIFFERENT NEEDS

Bible study for children is generally developed using one of three approaches: lectionary-based, theme-based, or comprehensive. Each approach has its own strengths and weaknesses.

Lectionary-Based Bible Study

A lectionary-based Bible study is designed around the Scripture selections (or lections) of the Revised Common Lectionary, a three-year preaching cycle that covers some of the major texts from each book of the Bible. (The three-year cycle is labeled as Year A, Year B, and Year C.) These Scripture selections follow the liturgical year: Advent, Christmas Season, Season After the Epiphany, Lent, Easter Season, and Season After Pentecost.

The lectionary has four readings each week: an Old Testament reading, a Psalm reading, a Gospel reading, and an Epistle reading. In most churches where the worship service and sermon use the lectionary, all four passages are used during the worship service. However, one lection is usually selected as the primary text for the sermon.

Lectionary-based children's curriculum is most effective when it is based on the same text that will be used in the sermon. Worship can be more meaningful when you have just studied the text in depth. Knowing who wrote the text, what was happening in the writer's life, and to whom it was written gives a background that is seldom possible in the short time allowed for the sermon. By studying the same material in Sunday school and worship, children can connect Sunday school and worship, experiencing them as one continuous event.

When all age levels—children, youth, and adults—use curriculum based on the lectionary, congregations have some exciting opportunities for learning. Families can continue the discussion during Sunday dinner, during family devotions, at bedtime, or during any other teaching and faith-sharing opportunity a parent might have with a child during the week.

While there are many positive reasons to take this approach, three major drawbacks make the lectionary-based approach difficult to use with children.

Preaching Texts

Lectionary texts are chosen for preaching, not for teaching. Many of the texts, particularly from the Old Testament, are difficult for young children to understand. Some of the lectionary texts are not appropriate for all ages of children. More often a small portion of the lectionary text is appropriate for children, but the entire passage is not. The selection of a text that is appropriate for even the youngest children may limit the depth of the sermon the pastor would like to preach, making it overly simplistic for youth and adults.

Which Text to Choose

As we said earlier, a lectionary-based children's curriculum is most effective when it is based on the same text that will be used in the sermon. Careful coordination is necessary between the worship leaders and the church school. When the preacher chooses to preach on a text that is not the text chosen for the children's curriculum, some of the benefits of lectionary-based Bible study disappear.

Important Children's Stories

Sometimes Bible stories that are important for children are left out when the lectionary is chosen for preaching and does not cover every passage in the Bible. Some important faith stories of persons responding to God's call will not be a part of a lectionary-based curriculum.

Cokesbury offers Whole People of God for all ages to churches that believe a lectionary-based Sunday school curriculum is the best option for their congregation.

Theme-Based Bible Study

Theme-based Bible study develops curriculum around topics (such as creation, covenant, or faith) or around groupings (such as the parables, healing stories, or the travels of Paul). In each case there are clear and logical reasons for putting together these biblical texts.

Theme-based Bible studies allow the students not only to learn the stories and their meanings, but also to see the individual stories as a part of a larger collection or theme in the Bible. This approach provides a framework to help children understand these teachings, therefore helping them to understand the rest of the Bible.

Some theme-based Bible studies may limit the number of stories children learn by offering the same stories in the same way. As children mature, they need to study new Bible passages that might not have been age-appropriate when they were younger. They can also begin to understand new themes in the same Bible passages they studied earlier in life. Any Bible study approach needs to cover Bible passages that are age-appropriate in order to be successful. A Bible study plan for children as they grow must also ensure that the entire Bible is covered during the child's developmental years.

Theme-based Bible study that has all ages (children through adults) studying the same topics at the same time has many of the same positive benefits as lectionary-based Bible study—conversations and reinforcement at home and with family. However, some of the same challenges of the lectionary-based Bible study also go along with this approach—making the chosen text and stories age-appropriate for children while still being challenging to youth and adults.

Comprehensive Bible Study

A comprehensive Bible study is based on a carefully chosen cycle of Bible stories that will be taught over the course of a number of years. Cycles are typically three, four, or six years in length and are designed to cover the Bible in an age-appropriate manner. In a comprehensive Bible study the biblical content and the faith development content are expanded each time the child studies the Bible passage. This planned repetition provides appropriate use of recall by the students, allows for discovery of new material, and uses creative ways for the students to express what they have learned. As the study covers most of the Bible during the cycle, care is also given to the church year and stories that naturally relate to one another.

Exploring Faith™ is Cokesbury's comprehensive Bible study. It is built on a four-year cycle, but the entire comprehensive Bible study is covered during the fall, winter, and spring quarters. Alternative studies are provided for churches during the summer, when many congregations look for "something different." *Exploring Faith™* incorporates the best developmental and learning theories to teach the appropriate biblical content at the correct age.

Adapted from *Why A Comprehensive Bible Study for Exploring Faith™?* © 2000 Cokesbury.

Your Bible Is What's in Your Head

by Nancy C. Zoller

Dick Murray, retired professor of Christian education at Perkins School of Theology in Dallas, says he used to think that his Bible was the black book with gold-edged pages that he could pick up and hold in his hand. But as a young man many years ago, he had a fox-hole experience; he was alone, isolated, and in danger. So he decided to pass the time and to overcome fear by reciting all the Bible verses he knew. He thought this would take several hours. But fifteen to twenty minutes later, he had completed his verses. Then he realized that his Bible was the Bible he carried within him, in his head. The rest of the Bible was still there; it just wasn't really his.

In the past students memorized the Gettysburg Address, Shakespeare, and the Bible. In today's world memorization seems to have fallen into disfavor somewhere in the 1950s, and now few people can recite verse of any kind.

Why Memorize?

Memorizing Scripture is not just for reciting; it's more than using rote memory. Murray says that in those fearful hours, the Scriptures brought God to him. The verses brought the God of rescue, of comfort, of peace, of consolation, of love, of redemption, of reconciliation, and most of all, of hope. The words brought him memories of godly people— his parents, his teachers, and his pastors—who had cared for him and had shown God to him. And the holy Scriptures in his mind and heart, even though only twenty minutes' worth, were able to drown out the voices of fear within.

The psalmist says "I treasure your word in my heart, so that I may not sin against you" (Psalm 119:11). God's Word bonded tightly to our hearts does keep us from sin. Jesus' words about a new commandment, to love one another, call to us when we are entangled with anger, loathing, or dislike. Christ's teachings throughout the Gospels call us to a higher plain than we can fathom on our own. Scriptural texts speak from within ourselves in the emptiness of our despair and confusion. And always, Scripture brings us good news: hope, forgiveness, and comfort.

That Was Then, This is Now.

Are we in the twenty-first century incapable of memorization? No! Just watch and listen to young teens in front of MTV or near a radio. They know every word of every song! Think of your three favorite songs. Now, mentally repeat

the lyrics. See? And can you recite the dialogue from parts of your favorite movie or TV show? Maybe they (and we) are not being challenged by schools or churches to memorize the phrases, statements, and verses that have shaped us as a nation, and more specifically, as a people of faith. Our teachers, and now we as spiritual leaders, are allowing our students' minds to be filled with secular, and sometimes even profane, texts with no spiritual content.

How can children handle the enormous number of belief systems, religions, and psychic claims that bombard them in our pluralistic world without a personal knowledge of the Holy Scriptures? What will bring them to God in the "foxholes" of their lives? Where will they find comfort and hope in their dark hours? So how can they get started?

The What.
Of the sixty-six books of the Bible (thirty-nine Old Testament, twenty-seven New Testament), where does one begin?

For yourself:
• Choose Bible verses that are most familiar and "perfect" to you, learning the reference (book, chapter, verse) along with the text.
• Select a translation to memorize. Today most of us read from the New Revised Standard Version or the New International Version, but some of us memorized verses as children from the King James Version. What makes more sense to you as you begin new verses?
• Pick one verse per week and practice it daily—not just once but throughout the day. Plan to silently repeat the verse on the hour of each day. Carry a three-by-five-inch card with the verse written on it until you can recall it without assistance.
• Recall all the verses you have learned weekly. Do this in the shower, in your car, while exercising, or while doing any routine task.
• Deliberately recite the Apostles' Creed without looking at the hymnal. Concentrate on what you are saying. Then begin to learn

another of the several creeds in The United Methodist Hymnal (pages 881-889).
• Intentionally set out to ask others —your pastor(s) and other laypersons—their favorite Bible verses, and add those verses to your list to be memorized. Often the older members of the congregation who did memorize Scripture as children will have many verses of personal meaning to share.

Seek chorus and hymn texts that are based on the Scriptures. Learn those as a way of learning the Bible verses and concepts.

With your students:
• Choose a translation for them. What version does their curriculum resource use? What Bibles do they bring to class? What text is most comfortable for them? Be intentional about the translation from the beginning.
• Examine the curriculum resource. What verses does it highlight quarterly? weekly? Select verses that connect theme and lesson
• Consider the "all-time favorites." What Scripture verses will connect your students to God's people wherever they may go?
• Look for and use children's songs, choruses, and hymns that are based on Scripture verses.

OUT OF THE BOX

The How.

There are three basics to memorization. The most basic "how" is repetition. Use every means imaginable to repeat the verse(s) you are teaching with your students. Remember that persons learn by hearing, seeing, and doing. Repeat the verse(s) aloud by reading from posters, by writing, or by organizing word cards (one word written on each) to proclaim the verse. Dramatize or sign the verses. Create tunes or sing to already-known tunes. Repeat the verse at the beginning and at the end of class time: by the whole class, by the boys, and by the girls. Create rhythmic patterns for the verses and add body rhythms like finger snaps or claps, or even stomps where appropriate. Ask your pastor or worship committee to include the verse during worship. Leave phone or e-mail messages for your students, repeating the verse you are studying.

The second basic "how" is motivation, sometimes called incentive. Create an atmosphere that affirms memorization of Scripture and celebrates the results. Enlist your pastor, church leaders, role-model adults, and parents in verse memorization.

Suggest that this month's verse is the secret code of your congregation and the way you greet one another. One person could greet another with "I lift up my eyes to the hills—from where will my help come?" The other could respond "My help comes from the Lord, who made heaven and earth" (Psalm 121:1-2). Participating in the secret code activity will encourage not only your class, but the whole congregation.

Offer some kind of recognition (ice cream party, doughnuts, pins, stickers, toys) for achievement. Arrange to have individual names printed in the bulletin or church newsletter.

The third and final basic "how" is recall. Resist the urge to move on to new verses too soon. Not spending enough time on verses allows those verses already learned to be forgotten by some children. Take time weekly to recall verses that have already been learned.

How Much Bible Is in Your Head?

Would Dick Murray's experience have been yours? Will it be your students' experience? Start now to make your Bible knowledge bigger so that you can sing Psalm 119:105: "Your word is a lamp to my feet and a light to my path."

From *Children's Teacher*, Vol. 7, No. 3.
© 2000 Cokesbury

Learn It by Heart

To memorize or not to memorize? That is the question! Do you ever find yourself wondering if you are doing your students a disservice by not having them memorize the key verse each Sunday?

Memorized words from the Bible can be a source of great comfort in times of need. Knowing the language of the Christian faith is important. And what better time to learn Bible verses that will stay with us throughout our lives than during the days we spend in our Sunday school classes as children?

But is simply memorizing the words of Bible verses really our goal? Certainly not! A much more meaningful way of learning may be the old term learn it by heart. To learn something by heart is much more than memorizing words. To learn by heart is to understand, appreciate, and even love the words we learn.

Remember these simple ideas to help your students learn Bible verses by heart:

• The best time to learn a Bible verse or passage by heart (that is, to memorize it) is while we are hearing the stories where the verses are found and exploring the meaning of those words for our lives today.

• The ease of memorizing varies among age levels and among individuals. Not every child should be expected to memorize the same verses or the same number of verses. Some children may even learn by heart more effectively by drawing a picture of what the verses mean than by memorizing the words.

• Use memorization as a group activity, allowing children with varying levels of memorization skills to be included.

• Children love competitive games, but be sure to reward children who learn what it means to "do to others as you would have them do to you" (Luke 6:31), even if they cannot seem to memorize the exact words from the Bible.

• Offer opportunities for the learners to be part of a loving community and to serve others as a way of bringing the otherwise meaningless memorized words to life.

Some Special Verses to Learn

For Younger Children:
• Psalm 23:1
• Psalm 100:1-2
• Proverbs 17:17
• Psalm 122:1
• Matthew 5:9
• Matthew 6:11
• Mark 10:14
• Luke 2:10
• Luke 2:52
• Luke 10:27

For Older Children:
• Psalm 23
• Psalm 100
• Deuteronomy 6:4-5
• Matthew 6:9-15 (The Lord's Prayer)
• Exodus 20:1-17 (Ten Commandments)
• Matthew 5:3-12 (The Beatitudes)
• Matthew 7:7
• Luke 2:8-14
• John 3:16
• 1 Corinthians 13

Exercise Eight:
Twelve Ways to Learn a Bible Verse

1 Ask several people in your church (pastor, choir director, parents, youth) to record the verse. Let the children guess who is saying the verse each time they hear it. Then let the children add their own recordings from memory.

2 Provide magazines or newspapers. Encourage the children to find pictures or stories that illustrate the verse they are learning.

3 Write the words of the verse on a chalkboard. Erase one word at a time as the children read the verse over and over. By the time all the words have been erased, the children should be able to say the verse from memory.

4 Have older children look up the verse in several translations of the Bible. Talk about ways the verse is similar and ways it is different in the various translations. Then have each student memorize the words that make the verse most meaningful to him or her. Don't forget to let the children tell the reasons for their choices.

5 Write the verse on a sheet of heavy paper. Cut the verse into irregularly-shaped pieces to make a puzzle. Let the children put the puzzle together to discover the verse. Challenge the children to time how long it takes them to put the puzzle together. Congratulate them for learning the verse well enough to put the puzzle together faster and faster.

6 Display pictures that illustrate a list of Bible verses. Let the children match each verse with the picture that illustrates the verse's meaning.

7 Sing the verse. If there is no Bible verse song in your curriculum resources, let the children make up a tune. Or they can practice singing the verse to various familiar tunes until they find one that fits.

8 Provide materials to use the Bible verse in a creative way. A simple bookmark with the words of the verse will help the children remember what they have learned. A larger bookmark with the Ten Commandments might become a craft item the children will keep and treasure even after they are adults.

9 Write each word of the Bible verse on a balloon. Include balloons with other words so that there is one balloon per child. Play music while the children try to keep all the balloons in the air. Each child will grab a balloon when the music stops. Those who have words from the Bible verse must stand and read the Bible verse aloud. Play the game several times, encouraging the children to put the verse in order faster each time.

10 Let the children illustrate a Bible verse with a picture they think shows what the Bible verse means. Have each child write the Bible verse across the bottom of his or her picture. Let the children show their pictures and tell what they illustrate. Have the children read the Bible verse together after each picture is shown.

11 Write each word of the verse on a square of paper or on a paper cut into the shape of a symbol that will be used in the day's lesson (cross, dove, chalice). Make several sets of different colors if you have a large group. Hide the words around the room. Once the children gather in the story-telling area, say: "Our Bible verse is hidden around the room. Each one of you may find a word and bring it to the circle." When the words have been found, let the children work together to put them together in a sentence that makes sense.

12 Write each word of the verse on a footprint cut from construction paper. Tape the footprints in order from the classroom door to the storytelling area. As children arrive, have them follow the footprints, reading the verse as they go. When all the children have followed the verse, call them together in the storytelling area to say the verse together.

From "You "Said "Yes," Now What?.
©2000 Cokesbury

OUT OF THE BOX

Tell Me a Story!

Children love stories! People have taught about God's love through the telling and retelling of God's story since ancient times. The people of God have come to know God's love and have been able to develop meaningful relationships with God and with one another as the stories of God's love have been passed down from generation to generation. Read Deuteronomy 6:4-9 for a wonderful biblical example of the faith being handed on to the next generation. Today, telling the stories of the Bible and stories about people of faith is an important way to help children learn about God's people and to develop a personal faith in God's love. As a teacher, you will want to develop your skills as a storyteller.

Try some of these ideas to help you become an exciting teller of stories:

- **Choose a story.** Before you tell a story to children, be sure that it is a story you know and love. Believe that the story you are telling is an important story for children to hear.

- **Set the mood.** Sit around a pretend campfire; wear simple costumes; lower the lights; use word pictures that help the children imagine the time and the place of the story. Perhaps you will want to ask questions to help prepare for the story. You might say, "Have you ever been scared? Listen to this story about a child who found out that it is okay to be scared." Help the children imagine that they are in the story.

- **Use your whole body.** Your facial expressions, your hand movements, and your voice will help the children feel the excitement, the sadness, the joy, the danger, the adventure, and the importance of the story.

- **Maintain eye contact.** Be sure that the children know that this story is especially for them.

- **Use dialogue.** Let the children hear the characters' voices.

- **Use lots of verbs.** Verbs are action words. Action will help the children experience the suspense and become involved in the story, wanting to know what happens next.

- **Get the children involved in the action.** Use motions or drama to let the children tell the story themselves. Don't forget the fun that comes from dressing in even simple costumes to play "Let's Pretend"!

- **Use visuals—especially with younger children.** Use storytelling figures or show the pictures in a storybook as you tell the story. Consider the props that will help children of all ages to get involved in the story. These might include a plate of vegetables to taste as they hear the story of Daniel, who refused to eat the king's rich food; a handful of straw to pass around the circle as the story of Jesus' birth unfolds and he is laid in a manger filled with hay; or a palm branch as you tell the story of Jesus arriving in Jerusalem.

- **Appeal to the senses.** Include sounds, and let the children make the sounds with you. Describe the smells, or even provide fragrances if the story calls for them. Talk about how things look, and encourage the children to imagine the scene in their own ways. Describe the ways things feel. Encourage the children to imagine what the characters experience as they feel the wind or touch the side of a mountain.

- **Repeat some phrases or actions.** Children may begin to tell the story along with you as they become familiar with the characters and the plot. When they can tell the story themselves, they will remember it longer.

- **Practice! Practice! Practice!** The better you know the story, the better you will be able to keep your attention on the students and tell the story with feeling.

Take advantage of your opportunity to become one in the long line of storytellers whose tradition of telling God's story began in the earliest days of God's people. Make the stories you tell come alive for your children. Make the stories they hear—especially the stories from the Bible—stories about real people that the children have come to know and love as they have participated in telling these stories.

Note that the word is 'storytelling'. When children ask to hear a story, they are not asking that you read the information about what happened to a character. They want you to breathe life into the story. They want to hear the characters speak and to hear the sounds of the story. They want to participate and become part of the story themselves.

From "You Said 'Yes,' Now What?"
© 2000 Cokesbury

OUT OF THE BOX

Ten Ways to Tell a Story

1. Be the Character
Dress up as a Bible character and tell the story first-hand.

2. Puppets
Let the children decide what the puppets should say and retell the story in their own words, using hand puppets.

3. Story Figures
Use cutout Bible story figures mounted on craft sticks and let the children do the movements as you tell the story.

4. Story Box/Story Mat
Place concrete items related to the story in a box. Bring them out and place them on a mat or the table as you tell the story.

5. Theater Box or Bag
Place various items of clothing in a box or bag and let the children take out the item, become the character, and tell the story.

6. Kamishiba Theater
Cut a viewing window from a box. Place picture cards inside the box that illustrate various scenes of a story. On the back of the card before, write the story so that you can tell the story and show the pictures at the same time.

7. Creative Dramatics
Read a Bible story. Divide the story into scenes. Divide the children into groups. Let each group choose a scene to act out in their own words.

8. Echo Pantomime/Movement
Say one line of a story or perform a movement that goes with the story. Have the children repeat that line or movement.

9. Choral Reading
Divide the children into groups. Give each group a part of the story. Let the children read the part in unison with their group.

10. Rebus
Write out the story on newsprint. Leave blanks for certain words. Substitute pictures for these words in the story. While reading the story, pause and let the children add the appropriate picture.

Puzzles Have a Purpose

Do you ever wonder if the children really get anything out of those paper and pencil activities? Just ask the children who love them.

When students solve puzzles, they will:

Practice Bible Skills
Knowing the names of animals in the Bible is not really the purpose of that crossword puzzle. The real purpose is to encourage students to practice their Bible-use skills. When the students complete the puzzle, they will know more about finding books, chapters, and verses in the Bible. They will have asked questions whether Leviticus is in the Old Testament or the New Testament, or where they can find the stories about Jesus. They will also have practiced reading the language of the Bible.

Remember and Review
Children (and adults as well, for that matter) learn through repetition. Our knowledge of the variety of learning styles tells us that children learn and remember things better when they experience them in a variety of ways. We may or may not remember the words to a Bible verse an hour later, for example. But if we complete a word puzzle where that Bible verse or a modern interpretation of the meaning of the verse is the answer, the information we get from hearing the verse will be reinforced as we discover the verse and its meaning a second time. Activities that help us memorize words are part of a plan that includes activities that help us understand what the words mean. The Bible verses and God's message to us through those verses become a part of our thinking that will not be easily lost.

Learn by Discovery
Students remember what they discover for themselves much longer than they remember things we tell them. Puzzles can be part of that discovery process. Encourage students to use puzzles to discover what Jesus said when he was asked to name the most important commandment. Then when you talk about Jesus' answer, students will be eager to tell you what they have discovered for themselves.

Enjoy Learning
Children enjoy crosswords, word searches, mazes, and other kinds of learning puzzles. It is a good thing to have fun as we learn about God's love and God's Word. Plan to use puzzles in ways that will encourage students both to learn the lessons you believe are important and, at the same time, to enjoy their learning experiences.

Let's Talk It Over

Times for discussion and conversation are important for building lasting relationships with your students. As you become acquainted with each child by listening to the child's deepest feelings and thoughts, you will build what may be a lifelong relationship. Even though you may never see a child again once he or she has left your classroom, the time spent talking and discussing important things will have an influence on everything that child experiences as he or she grows to adulthood. Long after a girl or a boy has forgotten the activities and even the lessons of Sunday school days, he or she will remember what you taught by your willingness to listen, understand, and guide.

Think of conversation—conversation that guides children's thoughts, feelings, and actions in regard to the main idea of the day's lesson—when you think of discussions with children. Discussion times are times that allow children to tell what they know, but discussions are also times for expressing important personal thoughts, feelings, and opinions. You cannot overestimate the importance of helping children know that what they think and say will be heard and that their thoughts will be valued.

Using Questions to Guide Conversation:

Some children are talkers. They will tell you everything they think, see, and feel without any hesitation. But even those children will sometimes need a teacher to guide the conversation in ways that help them think deeply and express feelings. One way to guide a conversation is to ask questions. But what questions are good questions? Think of questions in three categories:

• **Questions That Help Us Remember Facts**
These questions require only that the children remember the facts they have learned. Once a question has been answered, there is little if anything else to say. These questions will often begin with the words Who? What? When? or Where? Start a conversation with these simple, direct questions; it is important to help

children remember facts. Know that the answers will give children confidence and get them talking. But be careful! Too many questions that call for factual answers may feel like a test. Being tested does not lead to effective conversation.

• Questions That Help Us Understand Meanings

Quickly follow up questions about facts with one right answer with questions that help children understand the meaning (the important stuff) about the facts. These questions encourage children to think, because they may have many different right answers. These questions may ask "Why do you think . . . ?" You, as the teacher, may have your own opinions, but the many opinions of the students are valid too. Be sure that the students know that you are not waiting for a specific right answer but that you want to hear all the possibilities. These questions encourage children to think about what they have heard and then interpret what it means.

• Questions That Help Us Express Feelings

The most effective questions to help children learn to make decisions and form values are the questions that help them think like the characters in the stories they have heard. Saying "If I had been Moses, I would have . . ." helps children to understand Bible people. There may even be times when it is appropriate to ask personal questions, like asking about a time they were scared. Remember, though, that answering personal questions results in learning only when the child *wants* to answer. Never force a child to answer a personal question.

More Helpful Tips:

- Ask short, simple questions so that there will be no confusion about what you want to know.
- Avoid questions that can be answered with a Yes or a No.
- Remember that if there is no one right answer, there can be no wrong answer.
- Acknowledge every answer as valid, even if it is not the answer you were hoping for.
- Follow up answers that you do not understand or that you do not agree with by saying "Tell me why you think that."
- Concentrate on questions that stimulate the children's imaginations and provide opportunities for children to think and express feelings.
- Ask questions to the group. Do not direct questions to individual students until they are ready to answer.

When asking a question that asks for understanding and feelings, be sure to allow time for the child to think about his or her response. Be patient; thinking takes time. Even thirty seconds, a very short time to form an answer, may seem like an eternity of silence to the teacher. Allowing time for children to think will show respect for their opinions and thoughts while building their confidence in their ability to answer questions.

MOVING RIGHT ALONG: TRANSITIONS FOR YOUNG CHILDREN

by Elizabeth Crocker

Moving a class of younger children from one activity to another can seem like an impossible task. Because of the children's short attention spans and ease of distractibility, it can be a challenge to get the group to shift its focus from one activity to another. By the time the last child is ready, you may have lost the first one.

Transition times are the glue that holds the session together. Making your transitions meaningful and fun will create a lesson that holds together well and communicates your main idea more clearly.

It helps to understand that transition times can be stressful. Just entering the Sunday school room can be unsettling for preschoolers. They feel more secure once they are engaged in an activity. Slightly older children like to be allowed to finish a project. If it is worth doing at all, then it is worth finishing. Let the children know you are aware of their feelings. Reassure them that they will be allowed to finish their projects (and then make sure they have that opportunity). Be genuine and enthusiastic as you engage the children. Create a calm and purposeful atmosphere in the classroom. The children will find it easier to trust you and follow your lead if you seem sure of yourself and not scattered.

Younger children often need time to play and work until they are "finished." (This is one reason learning centers work so well with preschoolers and those early elementary children.) Because they function in the present, they are not likely to accept that they can finish a project later. They need a reason to move to something new if they are not finished with what they're working on at the moment. On the other hand some children will flit from one activity to another, sampling everything without thoroughly experiencing anything, or so it appears.

Eventually, though, the flitting child will likely settle on the thing that captures her or his attention. Be sensitive to the children's sense of timing. Let lingerers know when it will be time to move on. Say: "In two minutes it will be time to clean up." Let the children tell you when it is time for a new activity, as much as possible. Do not expect words. Watch their behavior. When you see restlessness or when materials are being used improperly, make a transition.

On the next page are some suggestions for making your transition times go smoothly. Try them as they are or adapt them to suit the needs and ages of your particular class. Many transition activities are often built into the lesson plans of the curriculum you are using. Remember that your primary purpose is for each child to know and experience God's love in your classroom. This knowledge is more important than whether he or she participated in every activity or completed every project.

Make transitions routine.

Most children, especially preschoolers, appreciate a certain amount of security in knowing just what comes next. That way they are prepared to follow instructions and listen appropriately. Many curriculums provide a regular lesson routine for each lesson. If yours doesn't include a lesson routine, you might want to create one.

Sing.

Musical transitions involve the children more fully in the transition activity. Music can also serve as an auditory cue. Engage the children as they move to a new activity, in one task such as singing that involves them in the lesson. And besides, it's fun. We want Sunday school to be a happy place.

Lead with a puppet.

Children like to play follow the leader. This makes a game of transition time. Leading the group to a new activity with a puppet keeps a key character before the children. This keeps the story alive as you move to something new. You can also use a child for the leader as long as you are methodical and fair in selecting leaders.

Provide visual clues.

Establish a signal that tells the children to stop what they are doing and direct their attention to you. Some common signals are raising a hand or flicking the overhead light quickly one or two times. Handling the Bible reverently and ceremoniously at story or worship time is a visual cue that tells the children it is time to listen attentively.

Use motions.

Walk in a different manner—for preschoolers you can tip-toe or stomp; for older children walk like the character in the Bible story. If there is an animal predominant in the story, let the children move as that animal. These actions make a game of the transition and involve the child's whole body, plus subtly getting the child into the Bible story.

Choosing Activities

1. Activity has a purpose in Christian education. It enriches the experiences of the unit of study and helps to fulfill the aims and purposes of the lesson.

2. Activities are planned with the needs, interests and capacities of the students in mind.

3. Activities include work with the hands, work with the feet in carrying out some service project, work with the mind in creating stories, songs, litanies, and prayers.

4. Activities often lead to rich worship experiences where children become aware of God and feel God's nearness.

5. Activities should be tried out ahead of time so that the teacher may be able to guide the children in carrying out a definite plan.

6. Activities should help the child discover deeper religious meanings and larger social relationships.

7. Activities should teach appreciation of others and give practice in cooperative living.

8. Activities should develop creative ability and help the child assume responsibilities.

9. Activities are best when both the student and teacher participate in planning them.

10. Activity is not busywork—never something to just fill in time.

11. Activities suggested in the teacher and student materials are planned to work toward specific goals in helping boys and girls grow in Christian ways of thinking, feeling, and acting.

Making Choices

Put a ✓ in each box that would be an appropriate activity for your situation.
Put a ✗ in each box that would be an inappropriate choice for your situation.

❑ Use fingerpaints to retell the Bible story.

❑ Write a litany of praise for worship.

❑ Play hot potato Bible verse.

❑ Wave scarfs or streamers to music.

❑ Make a get well card for someone.

❑ Brainstorm possible mission projects.

❑ Make a Creation quilt.

❑ Play with the sand table.

❑ Have a Bible books scavenger hunt.

❑ Practice writing the Hebrew alphabet.

❑ Make mud bricks.

❑ Dress as a Bible character and tell the group about yourself.

❑ Make your own paper.

❑ Read Psalm 8 as a reader's theater.

❑ Put together a Bible story puzzle.

❑ Decode a Bible verse.

❑ Make a paper plate shaker.

❑ Learn to sign a Bible verse.

❑ Learn to sign *Jesus*.

❑ Make a Bible character mobile.

❑ Paint a mural of the Creation story.

❑ Make a storybook for another class.

❑ Serve a meal at the soup kitchen.

❑ Collect canned goods for the food pantry.

❑ Make a class covenant.

❑ Create a code and share with a friend.

❑ Plant seeds and watch them grow.

❑ Make a paper mache' animal.

❑ Play with modeling clay.

❑ Sit quietly and think about God's creation.

❑ Write a haiku poem about God's world.

❑ Tell a story using puppets.

Mission Projects That Every Class Can Do

The feeling of wanting to be in service begins as soon as a child is aware that consideration for other people is necessary. How often we see children on the playground going to the aid of a fallen comrade. How easily touched are the hearts of preteen children who are suddenly aware of the needs of those less fortunate. As long as those of us who work with children nurture that spirit and provide avenues for the children to put their compassion to work, their spirit of service will grow.

The concepts for mission in the church are easily found in the Bible. Many passages tell about caring for the poor or the oppressed. Jesus himself set about to show the people how mission was to be done. Sometimes people get involved in mission as a way of seeing justice done. Others work to care for those who are less fortunate; still others see mission as a way of following Jesus' example and bringing others closer to Christ.

When we plan for mission activities, we need to gear the activities to the level of understanding of the child. Creating a service project for a four-year-old is quite different from designing one for an eleven-year-old, for example. The physical limitations themselves present a challenge for the preschoolers, and finding something challenging enough is an obstacle in finding service projects for the preteen.

Working with the 3s to 5s

Children at this age easily identify with others' feelings, particularly if the feelings they invoke are broad emotions such as happiness, sadness, or anger. Children learn to label emotions and thus learn how to incorporate helping behaviors. It is an act of service when a three-to four-year-old child offers to share a toy or a piece of equipment in the room. Sharing is hard for children at this age, because they often think they may never get the shared object back. As we teach the children to take turns and to share, we are teaching them ways to serve. Mission projects for this age group, then, should be concrete and tangible.

Working with the 6s to 9s

Preschoolers are possessive about things; six- to nine-year-olds are possessive about people. That is why children at this age feel rejection so acutely. Part of the goal of teaching mission and service includes showing the children that a person can have more than one friend and that people can work together to accomplish an agreed-upon goal. The self-centeredness of children this age makes it difficult for these students to perceive the world as others see it. Mission projects should help to expand their world view, opening their minds to others' perspectives.

Working with the 10s to 12s

Children in this age range are more able to participate physically in mission and service projects. They can also be more involved in making choices of just what to do. Give the children opportunities to talk about experiences they have and situations they see. Children at this age can contribute significantly when they are challenged.

Ideas for 3s to 5s

- Recruit families with young children to hand out bulletins for the worship service.
- Have children make a welcome kit for visitors to the classroom.
- Visit your community's sewage plant or garbage dump. Have the children take a token of thanks for the workers there.
- Have the preschoolers make a pastoral call to the pastor of your church.
- Have preschoolers visit a rehabilitation center for people with disabilities or the physical therapy room of a hospital. Talk about what we have in common with people who seem different from us.
- Encourage preschoolers to buy an extra toy for a needy child at Christmastime.
- Take flowers to parents after they send their freshmen off to college in the fall.
- Pair off with older children or teenagers to rake leaves in the fall. They won't get a great deal done, but they will experience the joy of working together.
- Have preschoolers sort and organize for a recycling project or donation collection.
- Make a class "We missed you" card when someone is absent from the group or class.

Ideas for 6s to 9s

- Make welcome pictures for new babies that come into the congregation.
- Visit homebound church members as a group. Bake cookies and take the cookies as a special treat.
- Adopt a specific military unit stationed overseas. Have the children draw pictures or write letters and send them through mail or e-mail.
- Make red construction paper hearts for each member of the congregation when the church is sponsoring a mission offering.
- Become partners with the youth choir to sing during worship on a specific Sunday.
- Have the children stuff a church mailing.
- Read aloud to toddlers and preschoolers. They can be book buddies.
- Make posters to advocate causes, such as recycling or donating to a food pantry. Hang these around the community.
- Hang a clothesline and attach paper mittens. Challenge the church to replace the paper mittens with real mittens.
- Clean out the craft supplies at the end of the year, testing markers and glue.

Ideas for 10s to 12s

- Collect back-to-school supplies for children who otherwise couldn't afford them.
- Collect soda cans, soup labels, cereal box tops, or other items that earn money. Choose a charity to donate the money to.
- Choose a specific missionary from your denomination. Learn about the country that missionary serves and find a way to serve that missionary.
- Invite a Red Cross representative to teach the children the basics of babysitting that are appropriate to their age level.
- Volunteer to wrap presents that have been purchased for persons in need.
- Create church partners with younger children. Encourage partners to seek each other out during congregational times.
- Organize a cemetery cleanup day.
- Make a commitment to serve a meal one to four times a year at a soup kitchen.
- Organize a cookie bake for college students who are away from home, particularly during exam times.
- Offer to put up and decorate Christmas trees for members of the congregation who are homebound or recovering from illness.
- Play board games with residents at a nursing home.

You can find many more mission and service project ideas in *Teaching Kids to Care and Share: 300+ Mission and Service Ideas for Children*, by Jolene L. Roehlkepartain.
© 2000 Abingdon Press.

Signing Is for Everyone

by Fran Porter

The noise of teachers and parents reverberated through the cafeteria. Kindergarten orientation made Casey feel as if he had a big lump in his stomach, and he felt very small. Then, across the room, through the groups of chatting adults, Casey saw his friend Heather from preschool. Here was someone who understood how he felt. Here was friendship and love. But she was twelve tables, forty-eight chairs, and a million grownups away. Casey lifted

his three fingers into the "I love you" sign they had both learned in preschool. Heather returned this greeting that came from a familiar time, and both of them smiled.

Language Learning Through Signing

Having taught American Sign Language (one or two signs a day to hearing four-year-olds in our church's weekday preschool) for over twenty years, I have found that signing enriches the lives and learning of everyone who comes in contact with it.

Signing broadens language experiences for young children at the peak of language learning and on the brink of reading and writing. The thinking processes for learning sign language are much like those needed to learn any language. Since these early years are the peak years for language learning, learning to sign is not only easy, but great fun for the children. It is exciting for the children to begin to transfer signs into sentences and into real communication. "More drink, please" is great fun to sign and respond to at snack time when passing the pitcher of juice.

In the process of learning sign language, children practice visual imitation of movement, improve small muscle coordination, and learn to keep thoughts in their heads without speaking them. Signing is a very quiet activity for a noisy classroom.

Try Finger Spelling

Elementary children expand language learning through finger spelling. Finger spelling uses a finger symbol for each letter, spelling out the whole word letter by letter. Sign language uses one symbol to represent the whole idea or concept.

It is fun for older children to create their own signs for their names. They will keep the finger symbol for their first initial while making a sign that tells something about themselves.

They might say "I hold my fingers in the F hand as I make the sign for *teach*. Then I rub my hands together like I am warming myself over a fire in order to sign *Methodist*." This is

the same sign as the one for *enthusiasm*.

A Communication Bridge

For both older and younger children, sign language becomes a kind of secret language that can bring recognition and comfort, as it did in Casey's and Heather's situation. The children enjoy teaching one another signs, and they also enjoy being able to teach adults something. Knowing how to make just a few signs can begin to bridge the language and understanding gap when hearing-impaired and hearing children interact. Participation in signing opens the door to better understanding, even if the communication is not interactive.

Some Signs Are Obvious

Teaching sign language makes the origin of some signs readily apparent. The signs for drinking and eating are just gestures of these actions, for example. Some signs are archaic, like the indication of a bonnet bow or a hat brim for a woman and a man, respectively. And some lead to deeper understanding, like lifting a hand upward toward heaven, then bringing the hand to the center of the chest to represent our God, who is in heaven and is the center of our being.

Kristy, one of our former preschoolers and now a talented high school senior, signed the words to "Thou Art Worthy" as she sang with our church praise band in worship this morning. As her fingers danced to *glory*, her eyes lifted in *honor*, and her arms flexed to show *power*, the truth of the words became clearer to me. I spoke with her after the service and shared with her my feeling that the sign language called me to worship as much as the sung words did. She quickly corrected me, saying, "More, it's more! It's more than words—better than just words; it's more!" Sign language *is* more. It's more than just words—better than just words; it's more!

_____

Fran Porter, who says "After twenty years, I still love to go to work every day," is director/teacher of the Deltona United Methodist Preschool in Deltona, Florida. She is also a long-time board member of The United Methodist Association of Preschools of the Florida Conference.

Exercise Ten:
Bible Verses to Sign

Ephesians 4:32

Be: Make the *B* sign. Move slightly right and left.

kind: The open hand is placed on the body above the heart. Move hand up, out, in, up, and around left open hand, which faces the body, pointing left.

to: Right index finger moves toward left index finger and then touches it.

one another: Circle the right *A* hand, which is pointing down, in counter-clockwise motion around the thumb of left *A* hand, which is pointing up and moving counterclockwise.

Psalm 37:3

Trust: Bring both hands to left, closing them to make *S* hands. Right hand should be slightly lower than left.

in: Place fingers of right hand inside the fingers of left hand.

the Lord: Place *L* hand at left shoulder and move to waist on right.

and: Place right hand in front of body, fingers apart and pointing left. Draw hand to right, closing fingertips.

do: Place *C* hands in front of the body, palms down; move hands right and left several times.

good: Touch lips with fingers of right hand. Move right hand forward, placing it palm up in palm of left hand.

Psalm 100:2

Worship: Place the right *A* inside the left curved hand; draw hands up and toward you in reverent attitude.

the Lord: Place right *L* at left shoulder, then on right waist.

with: Place *A* hands together, palm-to-palm.

gladness (joy): Open hands pat chest several times with slight upward motion.

Luke 4:18

The Spirit: Place right palm above and facing the left palm with fingers spread. As right hand moves up, index and thumb tips of both hands close.

of: Hook right index finger and thumb into left index finger and thumb.

the Lord Place *L* hand at left shoulder and move it to the waist on right side of body.

is: Move pinky finger back and forth.

upon (on): Place palm of right open hand on back of left open hand.

me: Point the right index finger at yourself.

Exodus 14:13

 **Do:** Place *C* hands in front of body, palms down; move hands to right and left several times.

 not: Place thumb of right *A* hand beneath the chin and move it forward.

 be: Hold palm forward, thumb down.

 **afraid:** Hold both *AND* hands in front of the chest, fingers pointing toward each other. Open both hands and move them toward each other, palms facing body.

 **Stand:** Place right *V* hand in standing position on left open palm.

 **firm (still):** Place index finger against mouth. Draw both open hands down and toward side, palms facing down.

Psalm 37:7, *Good News Bible*

 Be: Hold palm forward, thumb down.

patient: Place thumbnail of right "A" hand against lips and draw downward.

wait: Hold left hand, palm up, away from left side; hold right hand in same position near body with fingers pointing at left wrist. Wiggle fingers.

for: With index finger point toward the right side of forehead, circle downward and forward, ending with index finger pointing forward at eye level.

the Lord: Place *L* at left shoulder and move it to waist on right.

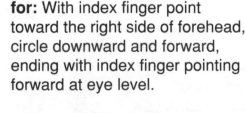

OUT OF THE BOX

"Hands-on" Really Means Hands Onl

Molding doughs and clays are not just for the very young. Even older children like to squish, mash, and squeeze them. Think of a super-active child in your class. Think how much energy could be siphoned off by giving her or him a handful of colorful dough to manipulate while listening or discussing. You would be surprised at how successful this activity will be. Here are some inexpensive recipes for you to try for your class. (*Don't forget to dye them bright and interesting colors. Or let the older children experiment with their own colors.*)

Baker's Clay

2 cups flour   1 cup salt
1 cup water

Mix together the ingredients until a soft, pliable dough is formed. Add more water if the dough is too dry. Add more flour if the dough is too sticky. Baker's clay can be baked in an oven (just like bread dough) at 300 degrees until the object is firm. Objects will even puff up like bread dough. (You can microwave this dough as well. Do it in short bursts, testing the surface hardness.) Spray the finished creation with acrylic coating; baker's clay will attract rodents and bugs.

Cornstarch Dough

1 cup cornstarch
2 cups baking soda
1¼ cups water

Combine all the ingredients in a pot. Cook over low heat, stirring constantly. Don't let the mixture stick to the pan. When the mixture looks more like mashed potatoes than soup, your dough is done. Remove the dough from the pot and place onto a clean floured surface. Knead the dough (when its cool) until smooth. This dough is particularly well-suited to making jewelry and ornaments because it is so white and soft.

Silly Putty

1 liter water
1 box Faultless starch
½ gallon Elmer's black label glue

Mix the water and starch together until dissolved. Add glue and mix well. To make the silly putty colorful, add food coloring to the water.

Cooked Play Dough

2 cups flour
1 cup salt
1 T. cream of tartar
2 T. oil
2 cups water

Mix dry ingredients in a large pan. Add liquid ingredients. Stir over medium heat until the dough pulls away from the pan. Add color with the water and knead it in after cooking. Spray nonstick coating in the pan to make cleaning easier. This dough is elastic and easy to work with. The oil will keep it from drying out too quickly.

Tools to Use

rolling pins	spools
cookie cutters	mallets
garlic press	forks
plastic knives	golf tees
potato mashers	toothpicks
nature items	chenille
graters	sticks

Soapy Dough

2 cups soap flakes
½ cup hot water
egg beater

Mix soap flakes and water in a large bowl. Add food coloring. Beat with the egg beater until evenly mixed. Gather the mixture into your hands and form a lumpy ball. Place the ball on a plate and shape it into anything you wish. When you are tired of your sculpture, just use it as soap in your shower. Soapy dough is great for making winter creations. With its chunky texture, this dough works best for sculptures where detail isn't important.

Sawdust Dough

1 cup sawdust
½ cup flour
¼ cup water
1 tablespoon liquid starch or white glue
sieve or piece of screening

Sift the sawdust into a large bowl, removing the larger chunks of wood that might result in splinters. Add the remaining ingredients. You may need to add a little more flour or water to make a good dough, depending on the texture of your sawdust. Stir until the mixture forms a big glob. Turn the dough out onto a floured surface and knead it until it is workable.

Helpful Hints!

Kneading the doughs is an essential part of each recipe. Not only does kneading insure that the ingredients are thoroughly mixed, but the children derive a great amount of satisfaction from pushing, pulling, and prodding a dough.

Knead cinnamon, vanilla, peppermint, or other flavorings into your doughs to give them a sweet-smelling fragrance. Be careful, though; the smells just might make you hungry. Add a little glitter to the dough for pizzaz as you knead it.

Let's Paint!

Paint doesn't always have to be the tempera kind that you remember from kindergarten. In fact, tempera is just one of the many different kinds of paints that children need to experience. Try some of these recipes in addition to using tempera, acrylic paints, and watercolors:

Three-Dimensional Paint

1 cup flour
1 cup salt
1 cup water
liquid tempera paint
plastic squeeze bottles

Mix together the ingredients in a bowl. Add liquid tempera paint until you get the desired color. Pour the liquid into a squeeze bottle. Squeeze the mixture onto heavy paper. The mixture will harden into a puffy shape. Create several colors. Let the children draw a picture and outline with puffy paint.

Face Paint

6 tsp. cornstarch
3 tsp. cold cream
3 tsp. water
food coloring
muffin tin or 6 film canisters

For each color mix 1 tsp. cornstarch, ½ tsp. cold cream, and ½ tsp. water in a small container. Add food coloring to each container to create the desired colors. Stir until well blended. Apply with a small paintbrush. This body paint is not only easy to make, but also easy to remove.

Make Your Own Watercolors

1 T. vinegar
1 T. baking soda
1 T. cornstarch
½ tsp. corn syrup
food coloring
small plastic bottle lids
paintbrushes

Mix vinegar and baking soda in a bowl. Add the cornstarch and corn syrup when the mixture stops fizzing. Mix well. Divide the mixture among three plastic bottle lids. For each color blend in a few drops of food coloring. Allow to dry. This process will make watercolor cakes. Activate the color by dipping a brush into water and swishing it over the dried color cake.

Salt and Starch Tempera Paint

2 T. powdered tempera
2 T. liquid starch
2 T. salt

Stir ingredients together in a jar until they are evenly mixed. The starch will give the tempera paint a very smooth texture. The salt will give it an interesting texture. Experiment with a little more and a little less of each.

Fingerpaints Are Not Just for Little Fingers.

Even the big kids enjoy getting their hands messy. But there must be a few ground rules.

1. Cover the work surface with lots of newspapers.
2. Wear old clothes or a paint smock.
3. Keep a dishpan or bucket of soapy water and an old towel handy for cleanup.
4. Clean up spills before they dry.
5. Use specially-made fingerpaint paper so that it won't tear when it gets a little soggy.

Starch Fingerpaint

2 T. liquid starch
1 T. powdered tempera

Mix starch and tempera paint in a bowl, using a separate bowl for each color. Mix well. Spoon the mixture onto the paper.

Cornstarch Fingerpaint

¼ cup cornstarch
¾ cup water
powdered tempera paint dissolved in a little water

Combine cornstarch with a little of the water in a pot. Stir until the mixture forms a smooth paste. Stir in the remaining water. Cook over low heat. Don't let the mixture stick to the pot. Simmer until the mixture is clear and thick. Cool. Divide the mixture into bowls and blend in the coloring. Spoon the mixture onto paper.

Flour Fingerpaint

½ cup flour
½ cup water
1 tablespoon liquid detergent
powdered tempera paint

Combine flour, water, and detergent in a bowl. Stir until ingredients form a smooth paste. Divide into separate bowls. Add tempera paint, one color per bowl.

HELPS FOR CHILDREN'S SUNDAY SCHOOL TEACHERS

HAPPY BIRTHDAY

_____
NAME

_____
DATE